Make the Right Move *Now*

Your Personal Relocation Guide

Identify what you want in your ideal location
and create a plan to get there!

Barbara M. Brady

Praise for *Make the Right Move Now*

My wife and I found your book to be highly valuable because it made us confront certain aspects of our relocation right off the bat. For instance, we were all gung-ho about moving south, but one of your exercises made us realize that for us, quality of life was not just about cheaper pricing and great surroundings; it meant very little without any of our parents close by. We think this is very important for our daughter, and are now looking for housing in New Jersey that is closer to our parents with plenty of green areas and good schools. Each relocation has its unique characteristics, and your hands-on book allowed us to discover our own needs and solutions. In utilizing your guide I felt we had our own relocation consultant by our side!

— Louis Lima, Director of Training and Network Services, Prudential Global Workforce Development, Freeport, New York

I love the relocation guide, Barbara! First, it helped me visualize more clearly exactly what I want. Then I began to see that I needed a deeper exploration of different places, so that if I chose to move I would know exactly what to look for, based on my most important values and firsthand experience. As a result, I have set up my business schedule differently so that I could travel regularly, and I have visited some really unique places in the last couple of years. In the back of my mind, I have an invisible checklist, helping me decide if I would someday want to live there, and why or why not. My options are continuing to expand, so who knows what I shall find around the next corner. With your guide I got clarity of desire. A precious and priceless experience. Thank you.

— Debbie Happy Cohen, America's Focus Coach and author of *Reach YOUR Stars!* ™, Tampa, Florida

Your relocation guidebook helped me realize that I am where I want to be. Most of my life I have moved on average every two years. I was starting to get itchy and thinking that maybe it was time to move elsewhere....new, more lucrative opportunities, shorter winters, etc. However, after doing the assessment, I realized that most of my needs are being met here and that I can use my current home as my "world headquarters" and continue to travel for fun and business....creating more work in warmer climates in the winter. Thanks for sharing your resources and wisdom.

— Ingrid Bredenberg, President of Human Resource Innovations, Western Massachusetts

The guide helped me structure my thoughts through insightful questions. In addition, documenting my thoughts allowed me to objectively look at and weigh the most important factors for me in finding a place that would satisfy both my personal and career aspirations.

– Lara Kelso, Senior Management Consultant, Scottsdale, Arizona

Well written, easily understood and explicit – gives one a lot to think about! This guide is most helpful in assisting one with taking a deeper look within themselves to make decisions in order to move forward or change what they are doing in their lives.

– Gerilyn Livermont, Caseworker, Social Services; Badlands, South Dakota

You always help me focus on the process versus the result and on what I want from my heart rather than comparing myself to what my peers are doing. You help me understand and appreciate my essence, which I think we tend to resist with the society we live in; we critique it too much, comparing ourselves to everyone, and I think most people go through life without realizing what their essence is. I think that's why I'm in a good space right now, I'm not denying my essence.

– Roe, Northern California and Connecticut

Make the Right Move *Now:*

Your Personal Relocation Guide

Address all inquiries to:

Barbara M. Brady
Barbara@mycoachbarbara.com
www.mycoachbarbara.com

Editor: Susan Snowden, Snowden Editorial Services, snowdeneditorial.com
Formatting: Bruce Mulkey, Mulkey Communications, brucemulkey.com
Cover design: Shonnie Lavender, shonnielavender.com

First Edition

ISBN 978-1-4303-1578-0

Printed in the United States of America

Publisher's Note: Published March 2007

Acknowledgements

Special thanks go to my parents, Carol and Jim Brady, whose love and confidence in me has made it easier to move to other places and create a feeling of being "at home" wherever I've lived. They have always encouraged me to write, and have been supportive of my various relocations, even if they didn't always understand them! I would also like to give credit to my late Aunt Connie, who helped me make my most recent relocation, to Asheville, North Carolina in 2002, with the words "Look at it as a one year adventure. You have nothing to lose."

Many thanks go to all those individuals who gave their time to tell their relocation story for this book. This guide is much richer as a result of their sharing. They include Roselee, Susanne, Larry, Helen, Joe, Steve, Michelle, Linda P., Sandy, Detlef, Martha, Tim, Bob, Linda C., Genie, "Bruce" and "Jennifer."

I want to thank those people who helped me put this guide into its final form: Shonnie Lavender of shonnielavender.com, who worked her magic on my original cover design, making it come to life; Bruce Mulkey, of Mulkey Communications, who patiently formatted the final version into its much cleaner form; and Susan Snowden of Snowden Editorial Services, for her wonderful job editing this entire guide.

I'd also like to acknowledge all those folks who gave me their feedback and/or support in writing this guide, including Peggy Pusch, Louis Lima, Lara Kelso, Ingrid Bredenberg, George Ward, Florence Ferreira, Debbie Cohen, Margot Zaher, Helane B., Claudia Zysk, Gerilyn Livermont, Bill Harkins, Julia Guirgis, Pam Humphrey, Nan and Bob Morrow, Tom Heck, Grace Kerina, Jim Pitts, Shonnie Lavender, Bruce Mulkey, Barbara Cerridwen, Elizabeth Barbour, Laura Anthony and all the other "FRs."

Table of Contents

Introduction

Whether you are thirty-five years old and have lived in the same town your whole life but feel a pull to be someplace else, or you're leaving a relationship at sixty and would like to make a fresh start, or you've been laid off from your high tech career at twenty-seven and want to explore the world before your next career move, this guide and workbook will help you or you and your partner:

- Identify the gap between where you are now and where you want to live

- Get clear on what you specifically want in your ideal place

- Recognize and work through any fears that may be keeping you from living where you want

- Learn how to find your ideal place

- Decide among two or more "ideal" spots, alone or with your partner

- Create a relocation plan that fits your needs

- Glean wisdom from the stories and advice of diverse singles and couples who've relocated successfully

If anyone had told me at sixteen that by the age of twenty-nine I would have lived in Switzerland, Arizona, California, and Japan, I would have been certain they were smoking some mind-altering drug. If I knew they would be right, I probably would have thrown up from fear on the spot at the mere thought of leaving my warm, familiar neighborhood in Framingham, Massachusetts, for places far away and strange. I was also certain at sixteen that my destiny was to be married by twenty-three, live close to where I grew up, and have three to four kids. That's what you did as a good Irish Catholic!

I decided to write this guide for several reasons. First, I have directly experienced the myriad benefits associated with living in different geographies, including considerable personal growth and perspective changes, and I wanted to impart those to you. Second, I am a big advocate of living your dream and not someone else's, which sometimes involves moving to a place that better fits who you are. Third, I think many of our societal domestic and international problems would be more easily understood and solved if each one of us spent time living in a culture that wasn't ours. Living in another culture begets humility, gratitude, and tolerance. Living in a developing or undeveloped country in particular helps to dispel the attitude of entitlement, arrogance, and ignorance so common in well-to-do societies.

So, here we are! This book is not concerned with the logistical or operational end of relocating, but with looking at relocation from the perspective of your health and growth – mental, emotional, physical, and spiritual. We will be looking at the power of place from the vantage point of values, connection, energy, and the senses. To that end, you will find quotes throughout this guide from people who've relocated for a variety of reasons. Interviews from some of them are found in Chapter 8.

If you are looking for a guide that is focused on employment agencies or headhunters to contact, cost of living indexes along with economic indicators, employment statistics and number of schools and hospitals per capita, this is not it. I do include a resource list where you can find some of this information elsewhere.

How to use this book

The chapters in this book build on each other to guide you through the relocation process, from deciding if relocation is right for you, all the way through to committing to an action plan to move to your desired location.

Where you begin depends on how far you already are in this process.

If you and your spouse/partner are trying to decide together where to live, I suggest you do the exercises in each chapter independently, then come together to discuss your responses before going on to the next chapter. The last section of Chapter 6 discusses how to negotiate a solution if you and your spouse or partner can't agree on where to live.

If you are not sure you even want to relocate, start with the quiz in Chapter 1.

If you are still not sure, continue with Chapter 2, "Assessing Your Current Situation."

If you know you want to relocate but don't know where, I recommend starting with Chapter 2 to be clear on your intention for relocating and the essence you seek. This will set a strong foundation for choosing the place that's right for you.

If you have already chosen more than one place you'd like to relocate to and need help in making your decision, you may want to jump ahead to Chapter 6.

If you've already decided on your ideal place and fear is the only thing stopping you, jump ahead to Chapter 4, then to Chapter 7.

Chapter 3 helps you get clear on what specifically you want in your ideal place.

Chapter 5 gives suggestions on how to identify where your ideal place may be, and where to get more information about it.

Chapter 6 offers a process to help you solve the dilemma of you and your partner not being able to decide between two or more places.

Chapter 7 describes action steps to make moving to your ideal place a reality.

Chapter 8 contains stories from those who've relocated. I've included these to give you a variety of perspectives and inspire you.

Chapter 9 contains quotes from those in Chapter 8 and others who've relocated. It includes comments on what they would do differently if they had to do it over again, and advice they'd like to share.

Chapter 10 provides resources to support you in your relocation process.

To get the most from this guidebook I highly recommend doing all of the exercises in Chapters 1-7 that are relevant to your situation. Don't shortchange yourself by skipping them. Some exercises will take longer than others. Pace yourself. Set aside at least thirty minutes or more to complete them, and find a quiet place where you won't be interrupted.

Relocation can be a major life stressor. You will mitigate your stress if you do your homework ahead of time; this includes making sure you are moving for reasons that add to your happiness and well-being (as opposed to running from a situation that will follow you). You also want to make sure that where you are going has soil that will help you bloom, versus soil that won't support who you are and what you want.

Now that you understand the purpose of this book and how to use it, let's move on to Chapter 1, where you will read about how I managed to relocate several times despite my fears, and you will take a quiz to see how appropriate a move may be for you at this time.

Chapter 1: Are You Inspired to Relocate?

There is a saying, "Bloom where you are planted." I say, "Plant yourself where the soil will help you bloom."

My story

When I was ten years old, I couldn't spend the night at most friends' houses in the neighborhood because I'd get homesick for my parents. It wasn't uncommon for a friend's father to knock at my parents' door at eleven o'clock at night, me in tow, saying, "I'm sorry to bother you, Mr. Brady, but Barbara wanted to come home."

That was over thirty years ago. Since then, my feelings of homesickness have been squelched by my strong desire to explore new places.

What began with a move to college sixty miles from home (with Monarch butterflies playing "kick the can" in my stomach) has led to relocations that included Switzerland for a college semester, Arizona for graduate school, Southern California for the weather, Japan to teach English as a Second Language and explore Asia, San Francisco for personal and spiritual growth, Massachusetts for more growth and re-grouping, and now, Asheville, North Carolina to live out a vision I created in 1999.

With each move I felt both excitement and fear. Sometimes I didn't know anyone where I was moving. Sometimes I didn't have a job. Twice, the native language was different from mine. Except for one time, I've always moved alone. With each move I always felt some fear, but managed to do it anyway.

One example is when I moved to college. As I mentioned, I was scared to death to be attending college just an hour from home. I went anyway, realizing I could always come home on weekends. Once I arrived on campus I discovered that the saying "out of sight, out of mind" was true for me. I was so busy *being present* to my new environment, meeting new people and having new experiences that I quickly forgot to be homesick. It also helped that my roommates were feeling the same strangeness and homesickness I was.

My move to Switzerland came about after I learned of a study abroad program through my college that I could do for a semester in my junior year. My thinking was "That sounds cool, why not?" I talked my best friend, Mary, into going with me. I was fearful the morning I left, and felt nauseous on the bus headed to JFK Airport from Providence College on a cold February morning. But at that particular time, I hated my life where I was. I was feeling cynical about boys, was a little overweight, and felt unattractive. I thought life couldn't be worse in Switzerland.

Once there, I became so immersed in the strange sounds of French, German and Italian, and the new smells and sights that *I forgot about myself.* I became a sponge, soaking up everything around me. Living and traveling in Europe, I felt curious and alive. My confidence grew and I started feeling attractive. Through experiencing the kindness of strangers numerous times, I realized that most people are good and we have more in common than not. I **fit** in these unfamiliar countries I was traveling through where I didn't speak the languages. I felt a unity, a strong sense that I was never alone, and *grateful.* The cynicism left me. I shifted 180 degrees. Now I loved life and felt like I could do anything. This feeling remained after I returned from Europe, and subsequent moves became easier because I had already "done it," and had a positive experience.

With each move I discovered the rewards of stepping out into uncharted territory. · As a result, I feel very blessed, both for the rich experiences I've had and for the amazing and wonderful friends I've made.

I truly believe that if I could make the shift from being that scared, homesick kid and teenager, uncomfortable even sleeping at a friend's house across the street, to being very comfortable living in a "strange" place, then *you can too, no matter how old you are.*

In 1999, I had been living in San Francisco for two and a half years. I woke up one day and intuitively knew it was going to be time to leave soon. Although I loved San Francisco, I just couldn't see myself living there long-term. I wanted to feel connected to and part of a strong community. So, lying on my living room rug, I closed my eyes and asked myself, "Okay, Barbara, imagine you were going to live someplace *long-term.* What would it have to be like to make you want to stay?"

Immediately I saw green rolling hills. I felt the air. It was fresh, cool, and smelled earthy. I pictured myself and others riding bikes into a small city. These people were wearing Birkenstocks or hiking boots with jeans. It felt laid back and slow paced. The people here were friendly and open. They valued connection, community, fun, the arts, health, travel, learning, and spirituality. Most of us knew each other. I saw ethnic restaurants and outdoor cafes. I saw myself hiking, running, and biking. I felt very connected. I was in a small city, imbued with nature.

Over the next two years I told a few people the vision of my ideal place. A few of them said, "That sounds like Asheville, North Carolina!" I had never been there. Finally, in 2002 I was ready to move and came to check it out. I visited in September and moved to Asheville that October. Overall, it has been even better than I originally imagined. It has given me the essence of what's most important to me: Connection with like-minded people. This feels like home.

If you wanted to grow a palm tree, would you plant it outdoors in Alaska? Or would you plant a cactus in Miami? While it's true that changing our external circumstances doesn't always lead to peace or happiness, it's also true that by giving ourselves the right soil – soil best suited to nourish who we truly are and who we want to become – we can grow and develop our gifts much more easily.

There is a saying, "Bloom where you are planted." I say, "Plant yourself where the soil will help you bloom." Are you living in soil that will help you bloom?

This guide is meant to help you decide if you're a good candidate for relocation at this time, and to walk you through a step-by-step process to determine what would be your ideal in the next place you live. It is a great fit for both single people and those making the relocation decision in conjunction with a partner or spouse. In the latter case, I recommend that each of you do the exercises separately, then compare notes before moving on to the next chapter.

Before reading on, take this quick assessment to help you determine how good a candidate you are for relocation. I developed this quiz as a result of my own experiences with relocation. The questions assume that there isn't anything major that's currently preventing you from relocating, e.g., a sick parent who needs your care.

Exercise 1-1: Relocation Assessment Quiz

Rate yourself on each of the following statements on a scale of 1 to 3:

1 = doesn't apply   2 = somewhat applies   3 = definitely applies

1. You don't feel like you fit in the geography where you currently live. _____

2. You've found it hard to meet and connect with people where you're living.

   _____

3. You hate the weather where you are. _____

4. You're feeling drawn to a particular city or area of this country, or foreign country, and are dreaming about what it would be like to live there (either awake or asleep). _____

5. You are drawn to living in a topography different from your current one. (For example, mountains vs. flat; oceanside vs. inland) _____

6. You're experiencing health issues where you live, which may include seasonal affective disorder (SAD), allergies, heat-related problems. _____

7. Things just don't seem to be clicking where you're currently living and you don't know why._____

8. You're feeling a strong pull to live in another culture, whether short-term or long-term (Native American, Thai, etc.). _____

9. Your values are different from most people living in your community. _____

10. The place where you're currently living is draining versus giving you energy. _____

11. The lifestyle of your dreams would be difficult to have where you live now. _____

12. You'd really like to move, but fear is keeping you from doing so. _____

Now, total your points to determine your score. Total score: _____

Next find your score in the table below then read the corresponding interpretation.

Score	Interpretation
12	Congratulations! It sounds like you're living in a place that's perfect for you right now.
13 to 18	You may be settling for mediocrity in your location.
19 to 24	You **are** settling for mediocrity in your geography. It's time to think about where you'd love to live.
25 to 30	Hello???!! Why are you still living where you are?
31 to 36	Start packing!

Note: If your score was a 3 for _any_ of the following questions: 1, 2, 3, 9, 10, 11 or 12, I recommend that you take a closer look at why you're living where you are.

You've just read my story and taken the quiz to see if relocating is a good option for you at this time. In the next chapter you will take a closer look at the specific positive and negative aspects of where you are now, and get clear on your intention for relocating and the essence you seek. This will set a strong foundation for choosing the place that's right for you.

Chapter 2: Assessing Your Current Situation

Should I stay or should I go now? If I go there will be trouble...
And if I stay it will be double...

— The Clash

The following exercises will help you get clear on what's working and not working for you in your current situation. It will also help you get clear on your intention for relocating.

Set aside an hour or two when you won't be disturbed. Find a quiet, relaxing space. Put on some music you love that gets you into the creative mode. Light some incense if you wish, or some candles. Turn off your phones. Then write down your answers to the following. Or create a visual collage in response to these questions with magazine clippings and/or drawings.

Exercise 2-1: Are you living in soil that is helping you bloom?

Example: When I lived in Massachusetts in the early '90s I loved being near friends and family. This aspect of living there gave me energy. In contrast I felt drained and de-energized by the cold, snowy winters.

Check one: Yes_____No_____Not sure_____

Write down what specifically is helping you thrive or giving you energy in your current geography.

_____

_____

_____

_____

_____

_____

Write down what specifically may be stunting your growth or draining you.

> *Once we sold the garden center and we were living in Westport full-time there wasn't the sense of involvement in community we wanted. Friends were one and a quarter hours away and cultural events one hour away. We didn't want to live like this. We made a few friends but it was hard to get involved...the New England standoffish thing.*
>
> **– Michelle, who relocated from Massachusetts to Asheville, North Carolina in 2006** (See interview, Chapter 8)

Exercise 2-2: Are you living in a home that is helping you bloom?

Sometimes the geography is fine, but our housing situation is not.

Example: When I first moved to San Francisco, the vacancy rate for apartments was less than 1 percent, so for the first year I lived at the Mary Elizabeth Inn, a place for women in transition. The positives included a few good friends I made there and the community feeling. The negatives included a lack of space (my room was 8 x 11 feet) and lack of privacy, as I had to share a bathroom with thirty other women. I knew I wanted to stay in San Francisco, and visualized my ideal apartment. I eventually got one that was even better than my vision, with clear views of south San Francisco and the mountains. It had a deck and was quiet, peaceful, and sunny.

Check one: Yes_____ No_____ Not sure_____

Write down all the specific *positive* aspects about your current living situation.

_____

_____

_____

_____

_____

_____

_____

Write down all the specific *negative* aspects about your current living situation.

_____

_____

_____

_____

_____

_____

_____

List the opposite (or positive) for each negative cited above, with what you *do* want.

Example: My negative above was "Had to share a bathroom." Opposite was "Have my own bathroom."

_____

_____

_____

_____

_____

Write what you can do to create each new positive aspect.

Example: For "Have my own bathroom" I needed to find my own apartment, or have a roommate in an apartment with at least two bathrooms.

_____

_____

_____

_____

_____

> *I want to die in this place…it just feels right. When we first got to the house we drove here and I just sat in the driveway and I feel I bonded with the house – sounds strange but Jim (husband) did the same thing. Things happened and I feel lucky they happened – the move to California and the house. The house is home.*
>
> *– Helen, originally from Czechoslovakia, who relocated from New York City, to Rancho Palos Verdes, California in the 1980s.*

Exercise 2-3: What is at the core of your intention to relocate?

Example: I moved to Southern California in the late '80s for the specific experience of enjoying sunny, warm weather year-round by the ocean. I wanted the feelings of freedom and fun that come with this kind of weather.

What specific experience are *you* looking for?

_____

_____

_____

_____

_____

_____

If you are looking for a "home," what does that mean to you? E.g., is it a place, people, a feeling, or all/none of these?

_____

_____

_____

_____

_____

_____

> *I always feel like this is home when I get back from a plane trip somewhere.*
>
> **– Susanne, who relocated from Newport, Rhode Island to Boulder, then to Denver, Colorado in 1998**

What is the essence you desire most in your ideal place? (E.g., fun, community, healthy lifestyle, rich in cultural arts, etc.)

Example: In 2002 I moved to Asheville after identifying that the essence most important to me at that time was to be in a strong, rooted community of like-minded people I naturally feel connected to.

_____

_____

_____

_____

_____

_____

Are you wanting something that's temporary_____ long term_____ forever_____ or don't know_____? (Check one)

What do you hope to get or have that you don't have now?

Example: It may be a feeling of connection, being in nature, great business opportunity, the ability to ski, or just to sit outside year-round.

_____

_____

_____

_____

_____

_____

_____

> *I had some friends from Vermont who were moving to Colorado for skiing. During school breaks I'd visit and ski. The lifestyle was very healthy. It was okay to be thirty something and not married. Everyone in New England was married with kids. I wanted a fresh start in a healthy environment where it was okay to be single in your thirties.*
>
> **— Susanne, Denver, Colorado**

Note: If you're *running from* something, you're certain to find it wherever you go. You get what you focus on. Make sure you are excited about *going to* something instead. Focus on what you're passionate about.

Is this essence something you can get where you currently live? Why or why not?

Example: After living in Southern California for three years, and being exposed to Japanese, Vietnamese, and Thai food and people, I realized I wanted to live and travel in Asia. I felt drawn to Thailand and Malaysia. The essence of my reason for wanting to go was to soak up the experience of the lifestyle in Asia. I wanted to be immersed in it – the food, people, smells, music, everything. This was not an essence I could experience living in Southern California. So when a friend of a friend who'd returned from teaching English in Japan told me I could probably get a job at his school there, it felt right, as I knew this would help me accomplish my objective and give me the essence of what I was seeking.

Check one: Yes_____   No_____   Not sure_____

_____

_____

_____

_____

_____

Note: Sometimes it's not so clear that you can get the essence you want where you currently live, or if you need to get it elsewhere. In this case, I think your heart knows. Pay attention to your feelings and where the energy seems to be drawing you. It's not always logical.

> *There are majestic mountains and great towns with tons of people in their thirties. You have to love to be outside. People are very physically fit. People look younger than they are; they have a healthy glow. Nobody smokes. Boulder's smoke-free. Denver's becoming smoke-free. People ski, mountain bike, run, hike…it's just a really healthy lifestyle.*
>
> **– Susanne, Denver, Colorado**

You've just identified the basics of what you want and don't want with respect to where you live. You should also have a good sense of the essence you seek in that place. In Chapter 3, you will be creating a vision for your ideal place that is specific, clear, and positive based on twelve categories of questions. Have fun!

Chapter 3: Creating the Vision of Your Ideal Place

Following are NINE STEPS that will help you create the perfect place for you. These steps were adapted from *The Path of Least Resistance* by Robert Fritz:

The best place to begin the creative process is at the end. Think about the final result you want with respect to the place you'd love to live.

Exercise 3-1: Start with a blank canvas

Start from nothing. Do not consider the past at all. Simply shift your mindset to visualize a blank canvas.

Exercise 3-2: Get clear on what you want

Get clear on what you want with respect to the *essence* of the place where you'd most like to live. By going through each of the twelve topics below, you will be creating your *Desired Reality* by picturing what you would like to see in its completed form. Make sure each response is clear enough that you would recognize the result if you had it. *Don't limit what you want based on what seems possible to you.*

Exercise 3-2 includes twelve specific topics from pages 18 to 40 to help you identify what's most important to you in all areas of your life.

(1)   Family/Friends/Community

(2)   Culture(s)

(3)   Lifestyle/Temperament

(4)   Work/Career

(5)   Spiritual Connection/Religion

(6)   Leisure/Cultural Activities

(7)   Finances

(8)   Physical Environment

(9)   Health

(10) Transportation

(11) Personal Connection

(12) Personal Energy/Body Check

(1) Family/Friends/Community: Who are the people in your ideal place?

> *There can be no vulnerability without risk; there can be no community without vulnerability; there can be no peace, and ultimately no life, without community.*
>
> — M. Scott Peck

Example: Being an only child, my definition of family expanded early on to include close male and female friends as my "brothers and sisters." I don't think someone needs to be related by blood to feel like family. In my ideal place the people form an eclectic mix of different age groups, professions, ethnicity, spiritual beliefs, and hometowns. These people are open-minded with a "Why not?" attitude.

_____

_____

_____

_____

_____

_____

_____

Do you view "family" as strictly blood relatives? What would it take for someone who's not a blood relative to feel like family?

_____

_____

_____

_____

_____

_____

_____

How open are you to making new friends? Do you view friends as strangers you just haven't met yet, or do you need to know someone for a long time before becoming friends?

_____

_____

_____

_____

_____

_____

How geographically close do you want to be to your current friends and family? How close is close enough?

_____

_____

_____

_____

_____

What kind of friends and community do you *ideally* see yourself with? Fill in the blanks. If it doesn't matter, write "N/A": Are these people…

- Friendly, open, or reserved? _____

- Creative or linear? _____

- Introverts or extroverts? _____

- Liberal or conservative? _____

- Conventional or unconventional? _____

- Artists, corporate types, homemakers, entrepreneurs, scientific types, academics, other? _____

- Ethnically diverse or homogeneous? _____

- Gay, lesbian, straight, or a combination? _____

- Do you see singles, couples, families, retirees, and/or a mix? _____

  _____

- Punctual or more relaxed about time? _____

- Direct or indirect in their communication style? _____

- More rational or emotional? _____

- Group-oriented or individualistic? _____

- Past, present, or future-oriented? _____

- Other? _____

When I go back home (New England), everyone is caught up in their little dramas in their cul-de-sacs. It's more uptight. I'm probably more chilled. New England has that rootedness and values and family. You grow up with your friends and stay in the same town and your kids grow up together. Part of me likes that. The West has this but it's eclectic. You really don't meet anyone who's from here. You're at dinner with six people and everyone's from a different state. I didn't find many Mexican restaurants or Buddhists when I lived back East. It was a huge culture shock when I moved here.

– Susanne, Denver, Colorado

(2) Culture(s): What culture(s) most interest you?

For example, Japanese, Chinese, Mexican, Italian, Brazilian, Peruvian, Nigerian, British, New Zealander, Indian, Ukrainian, Egyptian, African American, Native American, U.S. –Southern, New Englander, North Western, etc.

Example: I was not that interested in the Japanese culture before I moved to Japan. I saw living in Japan as a means to experience other Asian cultures I was more interested in – namely Thai and Malaysian. What happened was that I became very intrigued with Japanese culture and really enjoyed it. Through friends in Japan I also got a chance to experience other cultures, including Nepali, that I wouldn't have otherwise.

_____

_____

_____

_____

_____

_____

I was enjoying the way the Europeans did things. It wasn't convenient but exciting and kind of neat going to cheese, bread, and butcher shops. People didn't buy clothing off the rack with seven different sizes of the same thing. People expressed themselves through how they dressed, ate, how they shopped, where they hung out in the city…The rules and regulations in Munich added to my comfort. Everything fell into compartments and made it easier to integrate.

— Sandy, who relocated from Massachusetts to Germany in the 1990s
(see interview, Chapter 8)

(3) Lifestyle/Temperament

What size is your community? Is it a big city like New York or Chicago, smaller city like Kansas City or Charlotte, or more of a town feel like Santa Cruz or Taos?

Example: Before I moved to Asheville, North Carolina I knew that I wanted a small city or town that was walkable. I wanted to live within bike riding distance to this city. I envisioned a place where people wore jeans and Birkenstocks, a place that was slower paced than San Francisco and had a laid-back feel to it.

_____

_____

_____

_____

_____

_____

What kind of lifestyle do you want? Fill in the space.

Laid-back or fast-paced? _____

Materialistic or earthy? _____

Wearing jeans and sandals, or getting decked out? _____

Other?_____

> *I knew I wanted to move to the West Coast; I preferred the lifestyle there. It's more liberal. It wasn't the South. The cultural aspects appealed to me. It's the western lifestyle, very open, fulfilling the need for change that we wanted. I think I've become more of myself here, where in the South I was not myself. I can dress casually for work, be liberal and open, including about my relationship. In the South there were so many things I didn't like about the politics and people's attitudes toward race and things like that.*
>
> *— Joe, who relocated from Atlanta, Georgia to Seattle, Washington in 1996*

What temperament does this place have? (Please read below before answering.)

Example: In the book *Type Talk* by Otto Kroeger, the author says you can "type" cities according to temperament, based on the Myers-Briggs Type Indicator® (MBTI®). He gave the example of San Francisco being Extroverted, Intuitive, Feeling, Perceiving (ENFP) and Washington, D.C. as Introverted, Sensing, Thinking, Judging (ISTJ). When I read this, I had a huge "Aha!" I was an ENFP living in Boston, which is much more like Washington D.C. than San Francisco. No wonder I felt like a fish in the wrong pond! The next year I moved to San Francisco.

To determine your Myers-Briggs type, I recommend taking the online assessment at: http://www.keirsey.com. Click on "Take the Keirsey Temperament Sorter II." It costs about twenty dollars.

In the following descriptions, I've given examples of cities I think reflect each characteristic described. *Please note that this is based on my perspective and not a scientific study.* Descriptions were derived from *Do What You Are* by Tieger and *Please Understand Me II* by Keirsey. (Complete book titles and descriptions found in Chapter 10.)

In an **Extroverted city**, people would tend to be open, easy to read and know, would tend to share personal information freely, enjoy a fast pace, and prefer breadth to depth. They would tend to talk more than listen, be friendly, make eye contact, and initiate conversations with strangers. Examples of Extroverted Cities: Los Angeles, California; San Francisco, California; Denver, Colorado; Montreal, Canada; Cusco, Peru; Kuta on Bali, Indonesia.

In a more **Introverted city**, people would be reserved and private, listen more than talk, avoid eye contact, or minimize the time eye contact is held. They would need more time to think before responding, and prefer depth to breadth. They would also need more time to get to know you before forming a friendship. Once they're formed however, they're lasting. Examples of Introverted Cities: Portland, Maine; Nashua, New Hampshire; Washington, D.C.; Frankfurt, Germany; and Toronto, Canada.

In a predominately **Sensing city**, most people would gather information and make decisions based on one or more of their five senses. They would trust only that which could be seen, heard, tasted, felt, or smelled. They trust what is "real" and concrete. If they are also "Feeling" cities, they would tend to be oriented to the present and enjoy food and "the good life." Examples of Sensing cities: (Thinking): Boston, Massachusetts; Little Rock, Arkansas; (Feeling): Boulder, Colorado; New Orleans, Louisiana; Amsterdam, Holland.

In an **Intuiting city**, people would trust their sixth sense, or intuition, more than the other five senses. They are more interested in reading between the lines and looking for meaning in everything. They are more interested in relationships and possibilities than facts. They value imagination and trust their gut feelings. They are future- oriented. Examples of Intuitive cities: San Francisco, California; Santa Fe, New Mexico; Sarasota, Florida; Northampton, Massachusetts; Sedona, Arizona; Shanghai, China.

In a **Thinking city**, more value would be placed on logic, justice, and fairness. The same standard should be used for everyone. Feelings are only valid if they're based on logic. Thinkers are motivated by a desire for achievement and accomplishment. Professions in academia, the sciences, law, and engineering would be prevalent. Dress may be more formal and/or conservative. Education would be highly valued. Security and money may be more important. Examples of Thinking cities: Boston, Massachusetts; Washington, D.C.; Frankfurt, Germany; Zurich, Switzerland.

You can identify a **Feeling city** by the value placed on empathy and harmony. "Feeling" type professions, such as art, music, alternative healing, and various therapies would be prevalent. People will tend to be warm, and take time to talk with you. People may tend to hug more and dress for comfort versus looks. Feeling good would be valued. Feelers are motivated by a desire to be appreciated. <u>Examples of Feeling cities:</u> San Francisco, California; Santa Cruz, California; Asheville, North Carolina; Santa Fe, New Mexico; Portland, Oregon; Florence, Italy; Nassau, Bahamas.

In a **Judging city**, there is a desire to live in a more structured and orderly way. There would be a strong work ethic. In these cities, things would get done! "Work first and play afterwards if time allows." Emphasis is on the outcome versus the process. Deadlines are taken seriously and people would make plans in advance. Order and organization would be valued. <u>Examples of Judging cities:</u> Boston, Massachusetts; New York City, New York; Washington, D.C.; Chicago, Illinois; Detroit, Michigan; Zurich, Switzerland; Singapore, Singapore.

In a **Perceiving city**, there is more of a play ethic. "Enjoy the moment and finish work later if there's time." Emphasis is on the process versus the outcome. Options are left open, deadlines are elastic, and adaptation is part of the modus operandi. People would tend to be more spontaneous and make plans at the last minute. Disorganization may prevail and people would want to keep all their options open. <u>Examples of Perceiving cities:</u> San Francisco, California; Asheville, North Carolina; Rio di Janeiro, Brazil; Lisbon, Portugal; Galway, Ireland; Kathmandu, Nepal.

Now, based on what you learned above, what temperament do you want your place to have? Extroverted or Introverted, Sensing or Intuiting, Thinking or Feeling, Judging or Perceiving?

_____

_____

_____

_____

_____

_____

(4) Work/Career

Describe how your current work fits into the place you are visualizing. For example, is your work dependent on being in a particular location, or can you do your work from anywhere?

Example: As an intercultural transition coach, I knew I could live anywhere, since I work mostly by phone. I knew I wanted to work mainly from home with some time spent face to face with people outside the house.

_____

_____

_____

_____

_____

_____

Do you see yourself changing careers? If so, to what?

_____

_____

_____

_____

_____

_____

Where do you see yourself working? For example, in a corporation, from home, outdoors, or someplace else?

_____

_____

_____

_____

_____

_____

_____

> *I didn't seek out moves for the sake of moving or for interest in other cultures/countries. I was simply driven by my interest in growing professionally. If that required taking a job located somewhere else, I would go there.*
>
> **— Detlef, who relocated from Germany to Massachusetts**
> (See interview, Chapter 8)

(5) Spiritual Connection/Religion

How important is spirituality/religion to you?

Check one: Very_____ Somewhat_____ Not much_____ Not at all_____

Example: It is important to me that I live someplace where there is a diversity of religious and spiritual beliefs, and that this diversity is respected and embraced by an open-minded community. I also feel a deep connection between nature and spirituality, and it is important that I live close to nature, whether it's the ocean or mountains.

How do you experience your spiritual connection? List all that apply: by going to church, being with people you care about, being in nature; through art, music, sports, or some other way...

_____

_____

_____

_____

_____

How important is it that there's a place of worship for the religion you follow wherever you live?

_____

How would you prefer that the people where you live express (or don't express) their spirituality?

_____

_____

_____

_____

_____

> *We are not human beings on a spiritual journey. We are spiritual beings on a human journey.*
>
> *– Stephen Covey*

(6) Leisure/Cultural Activities

What do you see yourself doing for fun? For example, going to coffee shops, used bookstores, movies; making jewelry; belonging to a chess club, etc.?

Example: When I wrote the description of my ideal place, I visualized some specifics, including ethnic restaurants with outdoor seating, peach iced tea, used bookstores, a movie theater with international films, a tapas restaurant, theaters and arts museums and galleries. I also saw people hiking and running.

_____

_____

_____

_____

_____

_____

_____

What cultural and educational activities are important to you? For example, art and science museums/galleries, theater, plays, symphony? Continuing education at a community college or local university?

_____

_____

_____

_____

_____

_____

_____

What sports do you enjoy? For example, hiking, skiing, sailing, swimming, football, basketball, baseball, hockey, tennis, bowling, golf, rock climbing, etc.? Professional sports teams?

_____

_____

_____

_____

_____

_____

What volunteer activities would you like to participate in? For example, Hospice, Big Brothers Big Sisters, Habitat for Humanity, Meals on Wheels, mentoring kids, etc.?

_____

_____

_____

_____

_____

Restaurants! What kind do you like? For example, ethnic, organic, vegetarian, meat and potatoes, etc.?

_____

_____

_____

_____

_____

_____

_____

> *Factors we considered included…restaurants, fun things going on all the time, hiking, outdoor activities, the Blue Ridge Parkway being close by.*
>
> *– Michelle, Asheville, North Carolina*
> (See interview, Chapter 8)

(7) Finances

Do you see yourself living someplace where, compared to where you live now, the cost of living is (check one): the same_____ higher_____ lower_____?

If you checked "higher" or "lower," by what percent? _____

Example: When I moved from Framingham, Massachusetts to Balboa Peninsula, California in 1987, a studio apartment in Framingham on a busy street was more expensive than my share of the two-bedroom, two-bathroom house I rented, which was two blocks from the beach and had easy parking. I could also easily ride my bike to shops, restaurants, and a movie theater. By the way, the sunny, warm weather year-round was free! Easy decision.

What (if anything) would you need to change in order to be financially comfortable in your new place? For example, get a higher paying job, rent out a room in your house, raise your rates (if you're self-employed), etc.?

_____

_____

_____

_____

_____

_____

_____

> *The city (Cleveland) and airport are convenient. What you get for the money for a house is excellent compared to Chicago. I pay half the taxes for my house and half the auto insurance cost versus Chicago.*
>
> **– Bob, who relocated from Chicago, Illinois to Cleveland, Ohio in 1998**
> (See interview, Chapter 8)

(8) Physical Environment

What kind of flora, fauna, topography, and weather energize you?

Example: In Asheville, I love the fact that I can easily park downtown and walk everywhere due to the city's small size. I love seeing the Blue Ridge Mountains on the horizon. I love the green lushness of the flora here and the temperate weather. A slower pace is also more important to me now, and that's what a strong rain or wet snow brings.

Do you see yourself in a city, suburb, or rural area? _____

What's the ideal population? _____

What is the topography that most excites you? Mountains, desert, ocean, or

something else? _____

What weather gives you the most energy? Cold, hot, humid, dry, sunny, cloudy,

rainy, snowy? _____

What colors do you want to see? The blues and yellows of Miami, lush greens

and grays of the Pacific Northwest, or something else? _____

_____

How about the architecture? Do you prefer modern, historical, Spanish style,

Victorian, Cape Cod, Colonial, other? _____

> *I've always wanted to live in Seattle ever since the Bobby Sherman song when I was a kid... "The bluest sky you've ever seen, in Seattle, and the hills the greenest green, in Seattle..."*
>
> **– Steve, who relocated from Atlanta, Georgia to Seattle, Washington in 1996** (See interview, Chapter 8)

(9) Health

Imagine you're very healthy and energized all or most of the time.

What do you need in order to have the ideal health on all levels – physical, mental, emotional, spiritual? (Things to consider include amount of natural sunlight, dampness versus dryness, air quality, altitude, accessibility to high quality medical care and/or alternative health care, degree of mental stimulation, emotional and spiritual expression.)

Example: In the Boston area, I got bronchitis almost every winter. Having visited Miami and New Orleans, I also knew I would find it difficult to feel energized living in a hot, humid place. Instead, warm to cool, dry, sunny weather is most energizing to me, and where I tend to stay healthiest. Asheville combines temperate weather that lets me exercise outdoors year-round, along with some rain and an occasional snow that forces me to slow down and take it easy; good for my mental health!

_____

_____

_____

_____

_____

_____

_____

_____

In what kind of weather do you tend to stay healthiest? What type energizes you the most?

_____

_____

_____

_____

_____

_____

_____

What parts of the U.S. and the world have this kind of weather?

_____

_____

_____

_____

_____

Do you suffer from any health issues now? If so, describe:

_____

_____

_____

_____

_____

_____

_____

If you have health issues, what changes would make a positive difference for you?

_____

_____

_____

_____

_____

_____

_____

_____

_____

> *Tim wanted a town with good medical facilities for when we get older. St. Charles Medical Center started a hundred years ago and has a forty-five million dollar orthopedic center. We have one of the top knee and hip replacement doctors here. They're about to finish a thirty million dollar heart institute, and next year, a cancer institute. Some of the top doctors have come here to pre-retire and/or for quality of life.*
>
> **– Martha, who retired to Bend, Oregon**
> (See interview, Chapter 8)

(10) Transportation

Think about your preferred mode(s).

Example: When I moved to San Francisco in 1997 I knew I wanted a lifestyle that didn't require a car. I lived in the heart of the city, just a block from several bus lines and a twenty minute bus ride to the train, which ran up and down the peninsula. I was in a neighborhood where everything I needed was within walking distance – the grocery store, restaurants, movies, church. It made life feel simple.

List all your preferred modes of transportation, and when you enjoy using each. For example, subways, buses, walking, biking, moped, driving, flying, etc.

_____

_____

_____

_____

_____

_____

_____

_____

_____

_____

_____

_____

_____

_____

Rank the importance of each mode of transportation in the table below.

MODES OF TRANSPORTATION AND THEIR IMPORTANCE			
Transportation mode	Very important	Somewhat important	Not important
Bike			
Walk			
Subway or train			
Bus			
Boat or ferry			
Easy freeway access			
Primarily secondary road travel			
Airport proximity – within 30 minutes			
Airport proximity – within one hour			
Airport proximity – within two hours			
Other:			
Other:			
Other:			

We realized that for quality of life we wanted to be in a neighborhood, to be within walking distance to things...we also wanted a small airport close by.

– Michelle, Asheville, North Carolina (See interview, Chapter 8)

(11) Personal Connection

What is it about the place that you imagine feeling most connected to? Is it the people, the views, the smells, or a combination?

Example: In California I feel most connected to the feeling that "anything's possible," the big horizon, mountain views, sun, and smells of mesquite burning at restaurants. In Asheville, I connect with the warm, open, laid-back energy of the people, the layered blue mountain views, the lush greenery, the sweet sultry summer smells, as well as the visual impact of the leaves and flowers with the four distinct seasons.

_____

_____

_____

_____

_____

_____

_____

> *The minute we were flying over it (Seattle) we really liked it. We stayed at a B&B on Capitol Hill. It was an October fall day. I felt like I was home. Partly cloudy, you could see the mountains...city right on water...like a whole new world...liked the climate, the temperatures, no more humidity...fell in love with it the first weekend we came.*
>
> **— Steve, Seattle, Washington** (See interview, Chapter 8)

(12) Personal Energy/Body Check

How do you want your body to feel in this place ideally, and how do you want your energy to feel?

Example: When I visited San Francisco in 1996 I noticed how alive I felt. My energy was high and I felt excited. I walked fast, laughed a lot, and felt very open.

_____

_____

_____

_____

_____

_____

Note: Our bodies are wonderful intuitive barometers. Feeling good is often reflected by a feeling of openness or expansiveness in our body, accompanied by feeling energized and perhaps peaceful. Feeling bad is reflected by a feeling of our body contracting or a knot in our stomach. Our shoulders may slump. We may feel tired or flat.

> *Learn to read your own yes/no signals from your body. You need that in order to experience life in a maximum way…I get energy with yes and lack of energy with no…I feel heavy when it's not the place for me.*
>
> **— Genie, who relocated from New Orleans, Louisiana to Palo Alto, California in the 1970s** (See interview, Chapter 8)

Congratulations! You have just completed Exercises 3-1 and 3-2: (3-1) Starting with a blank canvas and (3-2) Asking yourself, "What do I want?" These are the most challenging of the seven steps.

Now you are ready to complete the process with Exercises 3-3 through 3-8:

Exercise 3-3: Clarify what you want in positive terms

Make sure each response you came up with from the twelve topics in Exercise 3-2 is *positive* and lists only what you want and *not what you don't want.* For example, for the Finances topic, you don't want to say, "I want to live someplace that's not too expensive" but rather, "I want to live someplace that's easily affordable." To be even more specific, you could say, "I want to live someplace that's easily affordable, where the median price for a house is $175K or less."

Now go through each response for the twelve topics in Exercise 3-2 to make sure each is stated in positive terms.

_____ **Check here** when completed.

Exercise 3-4: Make sure all the major components you want are there

Reread each of your Exercise 3-2 responses to make sure they include all the major components you want. If something is missing, add it there.

_____ **Check here** when completed.

Exercise 3-5: If you could have it, would you take it?

Test each of your twelve topics responses in Exercise 3-2 with the question, "If I could have that, would I take it?" If the answer is no, cross that item off your list. If the answer is yes for a particular item, formally choose the item by saying to yourself, "I choose..." For example, for (8) Physical Environment you could say "I choose to live in a city or town where I can easily walk to a beautiful beach."

_____ **Check here** when completed.

Exercise 3-6: Compare your current reality with your desired reality

Write down a description of your current reality as it relates to what you want (from finalized Exercise 3-2 responses). Just describe the facts without making them seem better or worse than they are. For each element under Desired Reality (your vision), list the element corresponding to your Current Reality. For example, if part of your vision is to "live in a small community with a population of fewer than seventy-five thousand" list the type of community and population where you're now living. "I now live in a large city of three million people." If your vision includes never having to scrape snow and ice off your car again, a "don't want," turn that into a "want." For example you may write, "I live in a temperate climate that's snow-free." Your corresponding current reality could be, "I now live in a continental climate where it snows at least five months each year."

CURRENT REALITY COMPARED WITH DESIRED REALITY	
Current Reality	**Desired Reality**
Example: I now live in a city of three million people	Example: I live in a small community with a population of fewer than 75,000
Example: I live where it snows five months each year	Example: I live in a temperate climate that's snow free

CURRENT REALITY COMPARED WITH DESIRED REALITY (continued)

Current Reality	Desired Reality

Exercise 3-7: Your ideal day in your ideal place

Imagine it's tomorrow morning and you've just woken up in the place of your dreams. Write down a detailed description of your ideal day in your ideal place based on the information you filled out in Exercises 3-2 through 3-6. Make it come alive to your senses. In order to more easily experience being in your ideal day NOW, as you're writing, ask yourself these sensory-based questions: "What am I seeing?" "How am I feeling?" "What am I hearing?" "What am I smelling?" "What am I tasting?"

_____

_____

_____

_____

_____

_____

_____

_____

_____

_____

_____

_____

_____

_____

_____

_____

_____

_____

_____

_____

_____

_____

_____

_____

_____

_____

_____

_____

_____

_____

_____

_____

_____

_____

_____

Exercise 3-8: Stay focused on the result you want; the "how" of obtaining those results will develop organically

Example: In 1990 I knew I wanted to travel to Thailand and Malaysia and spend at least a month there. I was focused on *how* I was going to do that, and started looking for people who wanted to travel with me for that length of time. A good friend told me I should talk to her ex-boyfriend, who was returning from teaching English in Japan. She thought I might get a job doing that myself, but I didn't have much interest. I don't have any desire to go to Japan, I thought. However, by keeping my focus on the *what* – traveling to Thailand and Malaysia – the organic *how* – teaching English in Japan – e*asily* arose. As bonuses, I loved Japan and got to visit several other countries in addition to Thailand and Malaysia.

Your job is to be clear on what you want, which places your focus on *results*. Robert Fritz, in his book *The Path of Least Resistance,* says we should ask ourselves what result we want to create. "The question '*How* do I get what I want?' is a question about *process*, not the result." Fritz says this is limiting as the answer relies on "what you already know how to do or can conceive of doing." The answer may come in a form that you do not know yet, as it did for me with the teaching job in Japan.

Gertrude Stein once said, "'*You have to know what you want to get. But when you know that, let it take you. And if it seems to take you off the track, don't hold back, because that is instinctively where you want to be. And if you hold back and try to be always where you have been before, you will go dry.'*" (*The Path of Least Resistance,* p. 70)

Congratulations! You have identified what the gaps are between where you're currently living and your ideal place. You've written a very clear and specific vision for your ideal place, and even imagined your ideal day there, in full sensory detail. You must be very excited! This excitement will help you successfully complete the next chapter, which is about identifying and moving through any fears that may be keeping you from moving to your ideal place.

Chapter 4: Addressing Your Fears

> *Courage is being scared to death – and saddling up anyway.*
>
> – John Wayne

FEAR stands for False Evidence Appearing Real. Having fears is totally normal. We all have them, though the shapes may be different. If you are feeling fear about a potential move or anything else in your life, it doesn't mean that something is wrong and that you shouldn't relocate or do whatever it is you're afraid of. Feeling the fear is the first step to realizing you are on the edge of or outside your comfort zone. What you do with the fear is what matters. "We cannot escape fear. We can only transform it into a companion that accompanies us on all our exciting adventures," says Susan Jeffers, Ph.D., in her book *Feel the Fear and Do It Anyway*.

Exercise 4-1: Coming to grips with your fears

The following questions will help you put any fears in perspective:

What do you have to *gain* by relocating?

List everything you can think of.

Example: When I moved to San Francisco in 1997, my gains included living in a city with beautiful vistas, personal and spiritual growth, becoming certified as an integral yoga instructor, and a short-term relationship that taught me about unconditional love. My world became much bigger by being exposed to new experiences and people. You may think you know ahead of time what you have to gain, but you just may find you end up with other "gems" you never dreamed of.

_____

_____

_____

_____

_____

_____

_____

_____

_____

_____

_____

_____

_____

_____

_____

_____

I realized that I could make a dramatic move like this, and do it successfully. So I now feel that if I wanted to (or had to) move somewhere else today (or in the future), I could do it. But I also found out how much I really did like and value living in the Massachusetts area. I think getting away for a while was good for me, and allowed me to see what it was like at another place and among different people. But it also made me appreciate more what I had earlier.

— Larry, who relocated from his hometown of Arlington, Massachusetts to Miami, Florida for three years and then returned to Arlington, Massachusetts in the early 1990s.

What do you have to *lose* by relocating? List everything you can think of.

Example: In the example I gave above, where I listed gains realized from my move to San Francisco, I would say that what I lost by relocating included financial stability, since I went from a corporate sales job to part-time entrepreneurial endeavors. At first, I also lost some personal space, as I went from sharing a 1000-square-foot apartment with one roommate to living in an 88-square-foot "dorm-type room" with thirty women on one floor, all sharing a large restroom.

_____

_____

_____

_____

_____

_____

_____

_____

_____

_____

_____

_____

_____

_____

_____

> *I did start to miss the change of seasons, and my family and friends. After a few years, the newness and the initial excitement started to wear off, and I realized that Miami was not a place I wanted to settle and spend the rest of my life (or at least the next many years).*
>
> – Larry, Arlington, Massachusetts

What's the worst thing that could happen if you relocated?

Example: Before pursuing the teaching job in Japan, I asked myself this question and thought the worst thing would be, "I won't get along with the other teachers or students and I'll hate it."

_____

_____

_____

_____

_____

_____

_____

_____

_____

_____

_____

_____

What is the probability of this worst thing happening on a scale from 1 to 10? (1 is not likely; 10 is highly likely)

Example: In the move to Japan I thought this would be a 2 or 3. I knew I'd be teaching with six other teachers and thought "I get along with most people. I'll probably get along with at least one or two of them."

What would you do if the worst thing happened?

Example: I thought, "If I'm that miserable I'll just break the one-year contract and fly home."

Can you accept the worst? Why or why not?

Example: I thought, "Yes, I have nothing to lose by going to Japan. I might have to pay for my return ticket if I came back early, but I could handle that."

_____

_____

_____

> *One of the things I made sure of before going was that Detlef was clear that if I didn't like it (Germany) we could move back. We set a time limit of two to three years. That was my back door.*
>
> **— Sandy, who relocated from Massachusetts to Germany**
> (See interview, Chapter 8)

What is the *best* thing that could happen if you relocated?

Example: In moving to Japan, I thought the best things would include having a lot of fun experiencing the lifestyle and culture in Japan, Thailand, and Malaysia; gaining a new perspective, meeting new friends, and feeling more connected to the world and myself. In reality, I received all these gifts and more. I had the added bonus of dating a sweet Japanese man for most of the time I was there. This was not something I expected!

_____

_____

_____

_____

_____

_____

_____

_____

_____

_____

How do your gains and best thing that could happen outweigh your perceived fears?

Example: Since the worst case scenario I imagined for Japan was easily solvable, (just by leaving Japan) the perceived gains and best things easily outweighed my fears.

_____

_____

_____

_____

_____

_____

Imagine that now you are a senior citizen or very elderly. Visualize two scenarios:

A. You never relocated when you had the opportunity. How did your life turn out? What do you feel happiest about? What do you regret the most?

_____

_____

_____

_____

B. You relocated when you had the opportunity. How did your life turn out? What do you feel happiest about? What do you regret the most?

_____

_____

_____

_____

_____

_____

Imagining yourself as an elderly man or woman, what did you regret the most – relocating or not relocating? Why?

Example: When I was asking myself if I really wanted to go to Japan, this was the key question. I quickly went through my perceived worst case scenario, as well as what I wanted to gain from relocating there. Then I asked myself, "How would I feel if I *didn't* go?" My answer, "I'd always wonder 'what if?'" I knew then that I had to go.

_____

_____

_____

_____

_____

_____

_____

> *Not having done it at all the rest of your life you would be kicking yourself saying, "What if I had, what if I had?" If it's the right time of your life and the right thing, you need to do it so you don't regret later that you haven't tried it. You can always move back; that's easy. It's taking the step out that you may perceive to be difficult, but it's not.*
>
> **– Helen, Rancho Palos Verdes, CA**

What might some of the negative effects be of not moving, when you are feeling called to move?

Example: This could apply not just to geographic moves, but career moves, relationship moves, etc. What happens when you are feeling called to move and not following the call is a feeling of being stuck. Licia Berry, a gifted spiritual teacher/counselor I've worked with, told me, "We get stuck when part of us knows the highest course of action and the other part ignores this highest course of action, due to attachment or fear. Examine your resistance to doing your highest good. It's like a car where the front wheels want to go forward and the back wheels want to go in reverse so you stay stuck. When all of your self is aligned with your highest good, things move and you don't feel stuck."

Negative effects could include a loss of energy, loss of confidence, resentment towards anyone you feel is influencing you to stay, and regret that you're wasting time. Also, the longer you wait, the stronger inertia gets, and the harder it may be to move in the future.

_____

_____

_____

_____

_____

_____

Exercise 4-2: Moving through your fears

List all your fears about relocating under the "Fear" column below, including those that may have already come up in this chapter. Under the column "Dated Action Step," write what would help you move through each fear, with a date.

MOVING THROUGH YOUR FEARS	
Fear	**Dated Action Step**
Example: I might not have enough money to pay the rent	Example: Save at least six months rent before I move by September 1
Example: I may not like it	Example: Take a trip there January 6-13 to explore the area and see how I like it

MOVING THROUGH YOUR FEARS (continued)	
Fear	Dated Action Step

Twenty years from now you will be more disappointed by the things you didn't do than by the ones you did do. So throw off the bowlines. Sail away from the safe harbor. Catch the trade winds in you sails. Explore. Dream. Discover.

– Mark Twain

You've now looked at your fears, which takes courage. Give yourself a pat on the back! If you still have lingering concerns, that's natural and okay. The main thing is that you feel ready to move forward anyway. But wait! Where *is* this ideal place you've imagined in full Technicolor? Chapter 5 will give you ideas and steps on *how* to find your place.

Chapter 5: Okay, Where is This Place???

If you've done the previous exercises, you should have a clear idea of what you want in your ideal place. But where is it?

Well, depending on your criteria, you can rule some places out by population, climate, and/or culture. Here are four tips to finding where your ideal place is:

1. Get a map and highlighter. Color in or put a push pin in all potential areas/places your ideal place could be.

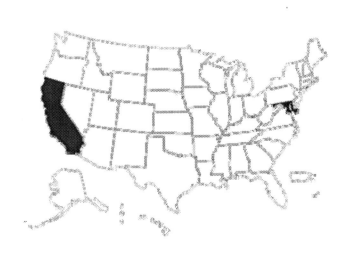

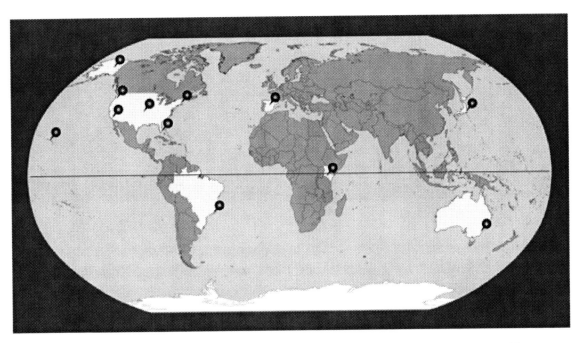

http://mars.jpl.nasa.gov/allabout/nightsky/images/World-Map_br.gif.

2. Start talking! Tell everyone what you're looking for, especially people who are living in or have traveled to areas you are interested in.

Example: I found Asheville, North Carolina when I described what I was looking for to a few people I met in my travels. After hearing my "list" they said, "That sounds like Asheville, North Carolina!" Talking with people will give you the qualitative information you can't get from a book or website, such as the degree of open-mindedness, values, and temperament of the people in general.

3. Go to the library or a bookstore and peruse books on the places you highlighted in Step 1. One of my favorites is *Places Rated Almanac* by David Savageau & Geoffrey Loftus. Visit the websites listed towards the end of this manual.

Example: In 1987 I was checking out Atlanta, Chicago, and Southern California before I realized the most important factor for me at that time was weather – sunny and warm. I went to my local bookstore and turned right to the weather chapter in the *Places Rated Almanac*. At that time Hawaii was rated #1 for weather. It seemed a bit far from Massachusetts. San Diego was #2. So that's where I went before ending up in Orange County, California, about ninety miles north.

4. Get personal. Go there! You will never know how connected you can actually feel until you experience the energy of the place yourself. In Chapter 7 you will find six ideas for diving or wading in.

Do you know where you want to move to? If you've chosen one place at this point that you are ready to check out, please go to Chapter 7. If you've identified *more* than one place, including with a spouse or partner, move on to Chapter 6, which offers exercises and resources to help you decide among two or more places.

> *My attention kept going to Nashville and Cape (Girardeau). There was attention, then desire to be in different locations. Started from subtle level of attention then desire. Then I started visiting Cape, and when I entered it I'd feel this happiness. When I'd leave Cape, I'd feel this pinch.*
>
> **– Linda C., who relocated from Asheville, North Carolina to Cape Girardeau, Missouri in 2006** (See interview, Chapter 8)

Chapter 6: How to Decide Among Two or More Places

This happened to me. Don't worry, you're not schizophrenic and you are not alone. If this should happen, I recommend you try one or more of the following:

Exercise 6-1: Grid exercise

Make a table with your places and criteria. Head each column across the top with a place, and list top criteria at the beginning of each row. Rate each place on how well it meets each criterion with 1 being "terrible, doesn't meet it" and 10 being "perfect." Add up the scores for each place at the end. The place that has the most points wins.

In the example below, Taos wins over Porto Fino by 2 points; however, you might also ask yourself how important each criterion is to you. In the real-life grid I created I had 10-15 criteria and 5-6 places. I also assigned each criterion an importance value from 1 to 10, and multiplied each place's score by that number.

For example, using the table below, if the "Feeling of connection" criterion was a non-negotiable for me, I'd give it an importance value of 10 and multiple that value by the score for each place. So Taos would have 90 points here, Ubud 40, Vancouver 60, and Porto Fino 20. Assigning each criterion an importance value will affect your final rankings.

MINI-RATING TABLE EXAMPLE				
Criteria	**Taos, NM**	**Ubud, Bali, Indonesia**	**Vancouver, BC**	**Porto Fino, Italy**
Near the ocean	1	5	10	10
Mostly sunny	8	7	3	7
Fairly small city or town	10	8	2	10
Feeling of connection	9	4	6	2
Ease of doing my work	6	3	9	3
TOTALS	34	27	30	32

MINI-RATING TABLE				
Criteria				

Exercise 6-2: Index Card exercise

Write each place you're considering on a separate index card. Now hold the index card with place #1. Imagine you are living there *now*. How do you feel? Notice how your body reacts. (From *The Purpose of Your Life* by Carol Adrienne, pp. 163-4)

Look for signs of "YES!" in your body, which could include the following:

+ Chest area feeling open and expansive

+ Stomach feeling calm or excited by butterflies

+ Erect posture

+ Body feels like it's plugged in or the electricity has been turned on

+ Lightness

+ Comfort

+ Increased energy

+ Corresponding emotions: relief, excitement, aliveness, peace, happiness, bliss

Look for signs of "NO" in your body, which could include the following:

- Chest feeling tight

- A pit in your stomach

- Throat closing up

- Heart contracting

- Slumped shoulders

- Feeling nauseous

- Pain anywhere in your body

- Feeling of heaviness

- Feeling tired

- Corresponding emotions: anxiety, irritation, disappointment, deflation, depression

Imagine yourself in place #1 six months from now, then one year from now, and notice how you feel and how your body's responding. Write down the feelings and reactions that came up during each time frame on your index card.

Do the same for place #2, #3, etc., until you're done. Which place feels best to you?

Note: If you are finding it hard to be aware of how your body is feeling, try learning what "yes" is for you first by saying something you know is true, such as "My name is_____." You should feel your body respond "yes" to the truth of saying your name. Now do the same thing, but say a name that isn't yours. Your body will respond with "no" to a falsehood. You can also see how your body responds to "yes" by thinking of people, places, situations and foods that you love, and then what "no" is for you by thinking of people, places, situations, foods, etc., that you *don't* like.

Exercise 6-3: The Coin Toss

Take a coin and assign heads to place #1 and tails to place #2. Toss the coin. Is it heads or tails? What is your initial gut reaction when seeing the result? What is your feeling? Excited? Disappointed? Is it a "yes" or a "no"? (From *The Purpose of Your Life* by Carol Adrienne, p. 164)

Exercise 6-4: Consult an astrocartographer

An astrocartographer is a professional astrologer who overlays your computerized astrological chart onto a country or world map. He or she can tell you what challenges you may experience and what aspects of your life might flow more easily based on location. (More information on astrocartography in *Resources* section at end)

Exercise 6-5: Map dowsing

This is a process of using a pendulum or dowsing rods with a map and a ruler to pinpoint a location. The dowsing tool is a "read-out" device for your intuition. To learn more, go to: http://www.hlla.com/reference/dowsing.html. I personally used this technique with great success before my move to San Francisco in 1997. At that time, I was considering several cities/states as options. A friend used dowsing rods to get a percentage of "yes" for each place. Most places were 50 to 65 percent. San Francisco was 95 percent "yes."

> *I was deciding between Miami or Seattle. I chose Miami because it was warm and tropical, and on the water. Also, the culture was exciting and different (a majority Latino). I had passed through there on my travels before, and had liked it.*
>
> *— Larry, Arlington, Massachusetts*

Exercise 6-6: When you and your spouse or partner don't agree

If you and your partner have done the exercises in each chapter separately, discussed your findings, and still can't quite agree on the place(s) to go to, I recommend that you go through the following six steps:

1. Write down all those things that *both* of you want in your new place. Start from the place of finding common ground.

Example: I want to live in a warm, sunny climate, and my spouse wants to live in a warm, sunny climate. We write these down as part of our common ground base. I also want to live by the ocean and he wants to live in the mountains, so we don't write these down here but will use these for the grid exercise next.

2. Do the previous "Grid Exercise" (Exercise 6-1) separately, listing criteria first from your combined list (from Step 1 here), and then individual criteria that are very important to you. List all the places that *both of you* are considering. Assign an importance value on a scale from 1 to 10 for each criterion, and multiply that by each place's score.

Example: Joan has seasonal affective disorder (SAD) and gets depressed in places where the sun doesn't shine. The "mostly sunny" criterion would probably get an importance value of 10 for her. If Joan's partner, Jack, doesn't have SAD, then the "mostly sunny" criteria might have only a value importance of 5 for him. Each location's score for "mostly sunny" would be multiplied by Joan and Jack's importance value.

3. Come back together and share your grid results. Find areas of compromise by determining how important each criterion is in making a decision for both of you.

Similar to Step 2, you would go down the list of criteria and ask each other, "How important is _____ to you? Non-negotiable, very important, somewhat important, or not very important? Talk about creative ways that both of you can have your non-negotiable criteria met, and/or other solutions.

Example: In the previous example of Joan having seasonal affective disorder, she may initially view a "mostly sunny" place as a non-negotiable. She may also ask what other ways SAD can be managed? There are special indoor lights that emulate the effect of sunlight, which could help. Joan and her partner could also travel to a sunny locale during the winter months.

4. Find areas of compromise by extracting the essence from what each of you wants.

Example: Zoë wants to live by the ocean. Jorge wants to live by the mountains. What do they do?

First, find out the essence of what each person really wants. For example, Zoë's main desire is to live near a clean body of water where she can have the freedom to swim when she wants, outdoors. She would also be happy with a swimming pool in the backyard or a clean lake nearby where she could swim. Jorge feels good seeing mountain views out his window. He doesn't care about hiking or actually being that close to mountains. This knowledge opens up more possibilities for each person to be satisfied.

5. As an option, you can agree to spend time in both places each of you has chosen. One way you can do this is by having dual residences (see Chapter 7). Another is by agreeing you'll live in one place, say London, England for two years, followed by the other's chosen place, e.g., Chicago, Illinois for two years.

6. If you still don't agree…you need to decide which is more important to you, the place where you live or being with your spouse or partner? This may indicate relationship issues you need to resolve that could be at the heart of your inability to agree on where you both want to live. I suggest going to a good counselor if you can't seek a solution on your own.

Okay! You may have narrowed your list of places to one, or you may still have a few places you'd like to check out. Either is fine. The next chapter will help you commit to one or more action steps that will get you to your place (or places).

Chapter 7: Creating Your Plan

Some people love to jump off the diving board to get immersed in the cold water at once. Others stick their big toe in the shallow end to test the temperature.

How you choose to "frame" your move will have a huge impact on your ability to overcome inertia and take action.

If you're thinking you must be absolutely certain before you make a move, then you'll never do it. It's natural to not know for sure.

Below are six commitment levels which range from sticking your toe into the shallow end with "Virtual Preview," to diving off the diving board with "Reality Commitment."

Read each commitment level below to see how it feels for you. Select <u>any and all you choose to do</u> by placing a check mark at the end of that commitment level description with a due date for completion. Be sure to choose at least one.

Virtual Preview

Search the Web for information on places you're considering. Some websites have huge photo galleries. You can often view a short video or see a "virtual tour" of your city as I just did of Vancouver: <u>http://vancouver.ca/aboutvan.htm</u>. Go to <u>www.google.com</u> and enter search terms such as "San Francisco, virtual tour," or "Virtual tours, cities" etc.

- Rent videos from your local library on the different states you're considering. (I did this and got 1970s videos on four states that were a hoot.)

- Get brochures from your local travel agency.

- Go to the Chamber of Commerce website for the town or city you're considering. Call them for a relocation package. These may be free or cost up to $15 – a lot cheaper than a plane ticket!

- Peruse the travel section at your local bookstore.

- Go to a travel bookstore.

- Talk to anyone you know who lives in the area you're considering to see how they like it.

- Let your friends and colleagues know what area you are interested in checking out. See if they have been there or if they know anyone you can call or e-mail who lives there.

_____ **Check here** if this step feels right.

Due date for completion:_____.

Reality Preview

Take a vacation to the area you're considering for a week or two. Try to hook up with a local who can show you around. Any friends in Vancouver? You can focus on just having fun and let your left, linear brain take a break. You are commitment-free and have nothing to lose. How much does the reality preview match up with your visualization?

_____ **Check here** if this step feels right.

Due date for completion:_____.

Reality Rental

Take a longer vacation, say a month or so, and rent a comfortable place, or house-sit for someone. Pretend you're living there and see how it feels. If you go to www.google.com and put the terms "professional house-sitter" in the search field, you'll get a list of services offering this. One site I found is: http://www.housesitters4u.com/main.html

_____ **Check here** if this step feels right.

Due date for completion:_____.

Reality Adventure

I got this one from my wise Aunt Connie. Make a short- to medium-term commitment to "trying out" this location. In reality you need a year to be able to give the fairest assessment of a location. Don't put undue pressure on yourself to *"have to know if this is the perfect place."* Give yourself a break! After all, what's a year in your life? How many years of your life have already blurred together because you were doing the same thing? It's okay if it's not what you want in the end. It doesn't have to be perfect.

_____ **Check here** if this step feels right.

Due date for completion:_____.

Dual Reality Adventure

Consider dual residences. Most of us know a few snowbirds who spend a few months in sunny Florida each year. Why not you? Whether you choose to live bi-coastally, as a friend of mine has done with homes in both Connecticut and California, or to live bi-nationally, as author Karen Kingston does with six months in Bali and the other six spent teaching and traveling in the West, get creative. In the twenty-first century, there are many occupations that afford us the opportunity to have multiple residences.

_____ **Check here** if this step feels right.

Due date for completion:_____.

> *I love feeling that I'm on vacation in both places...and also having roots in both places and having the luxury of doing work that is transferable (substitute teaching, sales rep, freelance work) and being blessed with two sets of friends...The minus is never knowing where your favorite book is, but it also helps you to let go and not get too attached to possessions.*
>
> *— Roe, who started sharing time between homes in Connecticut and northern California in 1998*

Reality Commitment

Okay, this is where you dive in and assume you'll be in your new locale for the medium- or long-term. You may do what friends of mine did who moved from Atlanta to Seattle, never having been there before. Within two days of arriving they bought a town home that they've now lived in for more than ten years.

_____ **Check here** if this step feels right.

Due date for completion:_____.

> *I sent Joe back out here to make sure the housing and everything was right. It was hard to let go of the past and move on. We were losing family and friends, moving three or four thousand miles away where I didn't know anyone but my partner. I made sure there were lots of bars near my house!*
>
> **— Steve, Seattle, Washington** (See interview, Chapter 8)

Choose

Remember that making no decision is still a decision. Decide which of the stages listed above appeal to you the most and put some body parts in the water! You can wade slowly into the shallow end, starting with the "Virtual Preview" and eventually swim to the deep end; dive right off the diving board with a Reality Commitment, or start by doing something in between. I recommend that whatever you do, it feels right for you and who you are. I also recommend minimizing any irreversible decisions as much as possible. For example, if you're planning to sell the home you've been in for twenty years to try a Reality Adventure or Reality Commitment elsewhere, rent it out instead. That way you can always easily change your mind later.

Get support

You can do this through a good coach, books, websites, etc. I also recommend telling a supportive friend which commitment level(s) you've chosen with the due dates, so she or he can hold you accountable.

E-mail me

barbara@mycoachbarbara.com I'd love to hear your story.

Congratulations again! You have not only identified where you may want to live, you now have an action plan to check out your place(s) within a specific time frame. If you are feeling in need of inspiration, the following chapter contains eight stories from those who've successfully relocated. And they're still alive to tell their tale! ;-) Sit back, relax, and enjoy entering their world...

Chapter 8: Relocation Stories to Inspire You

From New Orleans, Louisiana to Palo Alto, California

> *In California I feel much lighter. I'm not carrying a heavy steamer trunk on my shoulders.*
>
> *— Genie*

Genie completely changed her life when she relocated from New Orleans to California in the 1970s, transforming herself from a doormat to an authentic, inspiring leader. Genie is the president of *International Dialogue Education Associates*, a communication skills training company she created. She is also an author and artist with a Ph.D. in psychology. Now in her 70s, Genie has been living in Palo Alto, California for the past thirty years.

A petite woman with whitish-blond hair and penetrating blue eyes, Genie lives in the "flow" state that Mihaly Csikszentmihalyi describes in his book *Flow: The Psychology of Optimal Experience.*

She grew up in a southern Arkansas oilfield town. Finding it very provincial, Genie escaped at sixteen to college – LSU in Baton Rouge – where she eventually met her husband and moved to New Orleans.

Genie loved New Orleans. "It felt big enough, but everything was to make my husband happy. As I was approaching middle age I realized I wasn't happy because I had given up huge chunks of my identity to fit into the southern wife and mother configuration. In this role, I wasn't allowed to have opinions, and was quizzed on every action by my husband, who would tell me whether I could do something again or not.

"I had six children in eight years. The pivotal point was when I turned onto the streetcar tracks in New Orleans without looking left or right. I was staying for the children. I realized I had to leave because I'd be dead if I stayed and of no use to my children. The main thing was I was so unhappy, depressed. The last three years of my marriage were spent on the psychiatrist's coach at least three times a week. The psychiatrist said I'd been in a ten-year depression from a loss of identity. I had to be my husband's champion and rubberstamp everything he did. Being a rebel, it didn't work too well..."

On a trip to California Genie met a sculptor whom she befriended. He sent her a book on Esalen (a retreat center focused on experiential education and personal growth located in northern California), and she became intrigued with Gestalt psychology. In her forties, she went to Esalen for a week. "I learned more in a week there than in three years on the couch and ended up staying in California."

Once her older children were in college, Genie left her marriage and moved to California, where her youngest child lived with her until she left for school. Genie lived at Esalen for a year, then bought a house in Santa Barbara, where she got her Ph.D. in psychology. Then she met her second husband at a Gestalt group in Palo Alto and they later adopted a baby from Hong Kong. Genie's been in Palo Alto ever since. A major part of the relocation was starting her own business. She maintains her connection to her children and still has a connection to New Orleans.

"There's a whole different ambience about California. The energy is different here. When I'm in New Orleans I feel oppressed. When I'm in California I feel I can be myself. In Arkansas I feel even more oppressed. It's the narrow viewpoint, that rigidity of denying other experiences…tunnel vision…heavy atmosphere for me. In California I feel much lighter. I'm not carrying a heavy steamer trunk on my shoulders. It's a whole viewpoint, a different stance to the events of your life and the planet. More people here have open minds and are willing to grow, learn, and accept other people and their viewpoints even if they don't agree.

"I don't think I ever really decided to move to California permanently. I'm more spontaneous, doing things on the spur of the moment. I came here spontaneously and stayed spontaneously. I never made a decision to stay here long-term. I could leave tomorrow.

"As far as the future goes, we're not thinking about moving unless we reach a point where my husband and I couldn't work or something. No place else has called. And we really like our house."

From Atlanta, Georgia to Seattle, Washington

> *Go for it!*
>
> *– Joe*
>
> *I've always wanted to live in Seattle ever since the Bobbie Sherman song when I was a kid.*
>
> *– Steve*

Joe, in his forties, is an international vice president for a major advertising firm. His partner Steve, also in his forties, is a special education consultant/teacher. They moved to Seattle, Washington from Atlanta, Georgia in 1996 for a change in lifestyle.

Joe: I was feeling the need for a change, life was stagnant…plus we didn't really love Atlanta. We weren't passionate about it.

Steve: I was becoming tired of the South, tired of the racism. The school district was segregated; it wasn't open-minded. There was high crime in our area.

Nicknamed "The Director" in grad school for his "take charge" modus operandi, Joe is a guy who thrives on new challenges and travel. He grew up in Wisconsin, moved to Washington D.C. and later to Arizona for school. Then he met Steve and moved to Memphis, Tennessee, where he entered the world of advertising in 1986. A job offer for Joe brought them to Atlanta, Georgia, where they lived for several years.

Steve is a warm, charming southern guy who sees life through a lens of humor. He grew up in a small town in Tennessee, and lived in Nashville and Memphis after high school. Included in his eclectic palette are grits, ham hocks, and black-eyed peas. Joe fondly refers to him as "Grandpa" since Steve prefers hanging out at home watching Martha Stewart on TV versus jumping on a plane to Singapore for a good Indian meal as Joe would.

At first, Steve was reluctant to leave the South, but life with Joe has led Steve out of his comfort zone several times; now his travels around the world have included going on an African safari and trying all kinds of ethnic foods.

Joe told his company he wanted to live on the West Coast and they offered to pay for his relocation to any city there. Joe and Steve both fell in love with Seattle at first sight, and everything fell into place quickly.

Joe: I was open to any city and my company sent us here to check it out and we fell in love with it within the first twenty-four hours. I'd been to L.A. and San Francisco before; then we came to Seattle for the weekend, and it felt totally right. It was easy because I had a ready job and my company was going to pay for my relocation…we looked for affordability but Seattle was definitely cheaper than San Francisco. We knew we'd never be able to buy the kind of house we wanted in San Francisco but we could in Seattle. We fell in love with it; it was just the change we were looking for…we really thought we could see ourselves in this part of the country for a long time. I love it here…we love the cool weather instead of sweltering and using the air conditioner. We love having the windows open ten months out of the year and the fresh air. Considering how much I travel my life would be easier if I was living in Chicago or Houston – somewhere in the middle of the country. I give up a lot of time in order to live here.

Joe and Steve's retirement plans include living in two homes – one on Orcas Island, which is currently being built, and the other in their condo on Molokai in Hawaii.

Steve: I'm 100 percent satisfied with my decision to move. If you're fortunate and blessed enough to have two places in two climactic zones, why would you move? I think we have the best of both worlds.

From Asheville, North Carolina to Cape Girardeau, Missouri

Follow your bliss!

– Linda C.

Linda C., in her fifties, is a teacher and director of the Transcendental Meditation (TM) program for Nashville, Tennessee and Cape Girardeau, Missouri. Linda moved from Asheville, North Carolina to Missouri in 2006 to be with her boyfriend and to open up two TM centers.

Linda's petite, almost frail stature belies a strong, adventurous woman. She is warm, loving, and always has a smile on her face.

Linda grew up in Houston, Texas, ran the TM center in Houston, and at thirty-two, got her masters in Maharishi's Vedic Science (Maharishi, Mahesh Yogi, founder of the TM program) in Iowa. After graduating, Linda moved to Houston, St. Louis, Raleigh, and then Asheville to run the TM centers and teach full-time. In the spring of 2006 Linda moved to Cape Girardeau, Missouri.

"I wanted to see what direction my relationship with Tom (boyfriend) was going. I feel all of growth is based on change. When you feel the area you're in is not where you're supposed to be… although the environment in Asheville is beautiful, I felt it was time for a change. I checked my inner gauge. When I thought about moving to Cape and teaching in Nashville, I felt bliss. And when I thought about staying in Asheville, I felt non-bliss. I felt kind of flat inside. No stirring of any feeling. When I thought about moving, I felt this inner happiness, this feeling of excitement; that's when I knew I needed to make the change. The intelligence of nature that governs everything also governs our inner gauge. I feel when something is right, you feel "yes." If something's not right, you feel "no." I really tune into that when I make a big change in my life…I've made lots of changes and I always follow my bliss.

"My other clue was that my relationship with my immediate environment in Asheville shifted. Not in a negative way, but there was not such a connectedness. I think in our life we have certain responsibilities or interactions with people and environment and that's always for growth. Sometimes, these responsibilities are over; you've worked it out, and it's time to move on.

"Practical factors I thought of included: 1. Is this a place that's going to support me financially? 2. Will I find a place to live? 3. Also the environment is a factor. If it was a polluted place, no, but it's beautiful here. In terms of working in Nashville, I think the number one thing that attracted me is the population of one million. There's no TM center there; there's a lot of creativity, progress, expansion there. I thought it'd be a prime location to have a TM center.

"Before moving I visited my locations quite a bit (Cape Girardeau), looked for places to live, scouted the area before I made a decision. Same with Nashville, to see if it felt right, before deciding yes. I tied all the loose ends that I could possibly tie in my home environment in Asheville so there was nothing taking my attention there, and I had closure on a past romantic relationship.

"I'm 100 percent outer and 100 percent inner satisfied with my decision. I'm now more contented and just more secure knowing that I'm on the right course. Happy in the present and looking forward in the future. I've also noticed I take each day as it comes. It just feels exactly right. It feels easy here.

"In the future I'd move if it felt like it was time to move. Nothing is ever put in cement. Things are always changing anyway. Luckily I'm in a position where I can make the change. I don't own a home; I'm in a line of work I can do in many places; but I'm not thinking about that now, I'm very content; if there's a pull to move I'll look into that."

From Westport, Massachusetts to Asheville, North Carolina

> *When you're meant to be someplace you're supported by the universe.*
>
> — Michelle
>
> *If you feel right where you are, then everything else clicks.*
>
> — Linda

Michelle, in her sixties, is a Canadian-born entrepreneur. Her partner Linda, in her forties, is a former garden center owner from Pennsylvania. They met and lived in coastal Massachusetts before moving to Asheville, North Carolina in 2006.

Michelle and Linda are both down-to-earth, warm, open women with a good sense of humor. They went through a process similar to mine before deciding to move to Asheville: choosing five or six cities as possibilities, traveling to them, then comparing them to the criteria on their checklist.

Michelle: We realized that this (New England) wasn't where we wanted to spend the rest of our lives…the cold, long winters, no real ties other than a few friends; we wanted to live someplace warmer with a sense of community. People kept talking about Asheville, North Carolina. People we didn't know would say something about Asheville. Then a friend of ours kept talking about how wonderful it was…so we said "Let's go investigate." It was serendipitous. We started out looking for land, thinking we'd start building in two to three years. We came down in our RV for five days. We realized hilltop living was not what we wanted so we started looking in Asheville.

Linda: I had just sold my business, which freed me up, and I knew all along that Massachusetts didn't feel quite right. It never felt like home so I knew there was something else. It felt like the right time. It was tricky because I had to consider Michelle. It turned out we were both ready. I felt really unsettled, didn't feel grounded, didn't really have a very strong network of friends holding me in place. I was ready for something new and felt there were more opportunities elsewhere. When I was leaving there was this Shania Twain song with lyrics about leaving your job, transitioning, moving on. It was appropriate and I thought, This is my song.

Michelle: We'd also done a lot of traveling. We went to Utah last fall and thought of Sedona, Arizona, but there are water issues there, it was getting expensive, so nothing had really called to us in all our travels. We'd been to the West Coast, up near Seattle, thought of Nova Scotia but that felt isolating and it's still cold there most of the year. We asked ourselves, "Do we really want to be isolated?"

Linda: We found Asheville because we were looking for someplace on the East Coast. The West Coast seemed too drastic of a move. It was a process of elimination…New England was too cold, further south was Florida. For other tropical places I didn't feel comfortable relocating where I'd be a foreign citizen.

Michelle: Land was important to Linda. We had the gut feeling of "We could live here." People would ask, "What are the job opportunities?" We'd say, "We don't know, we didn't look. It's just a feeling."

Factors we considered included weather, community, and wanting to downsize, so the '20s bungalow was perfect, going to Jubilee (church) and seeing the sense of joy and community there, restaurants, fun things going on all the time, hiking, outdoor activities, the Blue Ridge Parkway being close by, having a small airport close by.

Before we relocated we researched and looked at houses in and out of the city. There was the synchronicity of the woman on the airplane from Charlotte to Asheville. She was extolling the virtues of a particular street in West Asheville. We got off the plane to meet our broker, who took us to the street next to where this woman lived. We fell in love with the house when we saw it. All the little pieces fell into place. The first house we put an offer on fell through; then something better came along.

Linda: We came with an open mind, positive attitude, and willingness to try it and see what developed…a lot of it is being open-minded, letting it happen for a little while, not judging it, and seeing what comes about. We're extremely satisfied with our relocation. I feel like I'm enjoying the living part of life rather than just the working part…right now I'm not working because I sold a business. I slow down and take each day and try to do something fun instead of work, work, work…If you feel right where you are than everything else clicks.

Michelle: We both feel so blessed. We listened to our hearts and guides and were open to possibilities. We have friends who want to move but they're not listening to themselves and are putting themselves in situations that are not ideal. It just feels very, very right. There's nothing missing now.

From Chicago, Illinois to Cleveland, Ohio

> *I'm a consultant so the whole world looks like my backyard.*
>
> – Bob

Bob, in his fifties, is a management consultant for a major consulting firm who lives in Cleveland, Ohio. He was born in Massachusetts and grew up in Washington, D.C.

Always moving for work, Bob has lived in New Jersey, Boston, Chicago, and Cleveland, where he moved six years ago to be close to both his work and his two sons, who were in Chicago with his former wife.

Bob is an optimist and high achiever. He is immensely curious about people and what motivates them. Spontaneous like a little kid, Bob lives in a state of wonder and excitement about life's possibilities. He also feels a profound sense of gratitude for life, partly the result of having almost died from an illness as a child.

I asked Bob, "Why did you pick Cleveland to live?" After extolling the virtues of the relatively low cost of living compared to other cities, Bob said, "After my divorce, my two boys moved to Chicago to be with their mother and grandparents. I was originally living in Chicago, but having to commute to Cleveland every week for work. Then I decided it would be easier to live in Cleveland and fly the kids in from Chicago or fly to Chicago myself to see them."

Before moving to Cleveland, Bob did his homework. "I was there every week for seven years before I moved there so I drove around to get to know the areas. I covered all the restaurants so I knew it better than Chicago."

Although he describes life in Cleveland as being "pretty good," Bob says, "I don't really have a home per se. My house is in a suburb of Cleveland, but it could be anywhere.

I'm a consultant so the whole world looks like my backyard. It feels like my neighborhood. I don't have a concept or sense of time and space anymore. When I get on a plane it's like getting on a bus. I've been to almost every major city in the U.S. and Europe. After awhile it collapses. I could find my way in most cities. I don't sense the same boundaries…San Francisco is like a block away to me. For others it's a once in a lifetime trip."

Bob is in the process of transitioning his work. "In my new career I might buy houses in different places: Hawaii, the West Coast. I belong someplace with a real dramatic view like San Juan Island. My house has to be on a cliff overlooking the ocean or something like that where I can get up everyday and be in awe."

From China to Houston to Boston

> *I'm a part of this culture – educated, culturally diverse.*
>
> *– Bruce*
>
> *I don't regret my decision. I love it here. I probably wouldn't have believed it eight years ago.*
>
> *– Jennifer*

Bruce and Jennifer, both in their thirties, are Chinese nationals and U.S. citizens who lived in Texas before being lured to Boston in 1998. Bruce is a software architect who co-created www.pubet.com to allow those who can't afford their own websites to publish information. Bruce's wife, Jennifer, works as an investment accountant.

Bruce is a highly curious, bright, and entrepreneurial man with a teasing sense of humor. His wife Jennifer is feelings-oriented, soft spoken, and feisty.

Bruce: I grew up in the northwest part of China, in a small city called Lanzhou close to a rural area. I went to college in northwest China and came to Texas when I was twenty-three in 1993 to go to grad school. I didn't know anyone. My younger brother and parents are still in Lanzhou.

To go to the U.S. I needed to get a scholarship from a U.S. university. Most Chinese students are poor and need scholarships to support themselves. I applied to twenty schools; two offered scholarships, including the University of Texas, Austin.

Jennifer: I grew up as an only child in Beijing, China. I came to Austin, Texas at seventeen with my parents. Father got a job at the University of Texas as a visiting scholar in the physics department. He came here in 1989; then he wanted me and Mom to come over to see Western culture and bring more perspective into our lives. We didn't know if it was long-term or not.

My first impressions of the U.S. and Texas were quiet, rural areas, like countryside. I was not prepared. I thought America was a big country with a lot of big cities and nightlife from movies…but not many people. In Beijing it's very crowded, people everywhere. People I met in Austin were very friendly. There was hospitality. I hardly experienced this living in Beijing.

Bruce: My first impression of the States was that most people are very friendly. I hardly spoke English then. I had no money. An American professor lent me five hundred dollars. America is a very clean, very rich society. I went to a supermarket and was amazed at all the different foods and goods. You rarely see those things in China except in big cities with larger supermarkets. There are so many cars; you can hardly move without a car. This was inconvenient because I had no car or money to buy a car. In China, most people go everyplace by bike, and everything is close. Here, everyone is so far apart; you have to take the bus here…the bus felt spacious; there was air conditioning, and it was not crowded.

I got my masters and Ph.D. in MIS (management information systems) and met Jennifer, who was an undergrad student. We married in 1997 in Texas. I was working for a big computer company. It was the beginning of the internet bubble. An Internet start-up in Boston found me, and gave me a good benefit package, so we moved here in 1998. We had no kids and it seemed like a good opportunity. They went bankrupt in a few years.

Jennifer: Bruce got a job in Boston and this company got his green card. We thought about how expensive Boston could be. It's a strange city, and at first I hesitated a bit. We had lots of friends in Texas. It was sad to leave them and cut off that kind of connection. It was a coincidence that a couple of friends from church in Texas came to Boston a month before us. This made it easier for us.

Bruce: If you lived during the Internet period, everyone was excited about the Internet start-up success story; They wanted to become part of that. There was not one defining moment for relocating but it was a process – you read the newspaper, watch TV with friends, we're all excited about the opportunities. I had offers from Amazon. I went to Seattle for three days, but didn't like it because it rained the whole time. I saw in the newspaper that only a hundred days every year are sunny. I had friends in Silicon Valley but no offers. I Interviewed in Boston; exciting town. I went to Harvard, MIT, Boston Harbor, and Cambridge. Lots of hippies and yuppies, different ethnic groups. I felt, "I'm a part of this culture" – educated, culturally diverse.

Jennifer: I quit my job to follow him over here. It never occurred to me whether or not I would find a job or what kind of life I could be facing. I did cry my first night here. It was very shameful, an emotional moment. We got here at the end of October. In Texas October is the nicest month in the year, very easy. When we got to Boston it was late at night, dark and very, very cold. We got in a taxi, drove through the city to Cambridge to our temporary lodging and all of a sudden I felt very sad. I can't imagine me making such a decision to move so far from my friends. I called Mom and appeared to be strong and positive. Then I called my best friend and burst into tears.

Bruce: I think it's a very good decision to move here. The downside with Massachusetts is that everything is more expensive than Texas in terms of housing, and there's the commute. The upside is it's a very historical town, with a good education system, and you can get information quickly. It's an intellectual hub here.

Jennifer: People are much more aggressive here than in Texas, especially in companies. Texas is more laid back, cowboy style, very straightforward. Here I've worked in the financial software and pharmaceutical industries. People are more into climbing the corporate ladder. I've met a lot of workaholics here. And the traffic! Texas is very easy and light. Construction there is new so highways are well built, as opposed to Boston, where people drive like crazy, fight over lanes, and beep if you slow down. The Big Dig in Boston was not a picnic at all when we first came and the cost of living is another thing. In Texas the cost of living is so much less than that of Boston. I was shocked at the price for a single family house, but now I'm used to it.

Bruce: Now I'm older, mature…I have a wiser view of the Internet and technology sector and how it's changed. I met my wife here; I have a child here now. I'm financially in a good position, and have friends here.

Jennifer: I really love it here. Massachusetts is a great state. There are four seasons and the scenery is wonderful. We're lucky we met so many good friends here. We have nice neighbors, and over time we achieved things: green card, different jobs. I completed my MBA; I had Emily (daughter). Living in Boston this past eight years is full of good memories. I don't regret my decision. I love it here. I probably wouldn't have believed it eight years ago. I've become more independent. I used to live very close to my parents. I went there all the time and living with them made me feel like I was still their child. The fact that now I'm thousands of miles away I feel I have truly grown up and matured a lot. I really believe when God closes the door somewhere he opens the window. Now I know if there's another opportunity I wouldn't be afraid because somehow it would work out.

From Germany to Massachusetts to Germany and Back to Massachusetts

> *You may not always agree but you develop an open mind.*
>
> *— Detlef, on living in the U.S.*
>
> *It was like I came from Kodachrome to black and white.*
>
> *— Sandy, on her move back to the U.S. after living in Germany for ten years*

Detlef, in his fifties, is a senior manager for a high tech company in Massachusetts and a self-proclaimed "German Waffler." Years ago he moved from his native Germany to Massachusetts, where he met and married Sandy. They then moved to Munich, Germany for ten years and back to Massachusetts in 1999. Sandy, in her forties, from Framingham, Massachusetts, is a "no longer working sales professional garden diva."

Detlef grew up in Hanover, Germany and went to school for engineering. A "thinker" and inquisitive by nature, he lovers intellectual discussions and has a mischievous sense of humor.

Sandy is an intelligent, creative woman who is a "feeler." Sandy loves to laugh and is a superb cook.

Both Sandy and Detlef "work to live" and believe life is to be enjoyed. They've made cooking and eating delicious meals an important event, along with appreciating good wine, friends, golf, boating, conversation, and travel.

Detlef: I came to the states when I was thirty-one. I was presenting myself as someone who was willing and able and eager to do what it takes. I worked my ass off to do a good job…whenever I take a new job I just work hard, go the extra mile, and do research to get a clear read on the new place. I'd meet with my future boss and visit the office in the new city…

On his move to the U.S.
Detlef: I think the U.S. move changed my life – I got married here…getting involved and integrated in another society/culture is obviously an enrichment. It gives you a different perspective on things and it's something that I wouldn't have wanted to miss. It makes you a totally different person. Just think about it, if you're really

comfortable and fluent in two different languages…to be really fluent, you need to be fluent in that society and culture. That makes you a different person. It definitely makes you open to new things and just by having to absorb the multiple ways of doing things and looking at things, you may not always agree but you develop an open mind automatically – not everyone, some people are set in their ways, but they can't be successful. Not that you buy into everything, but you have to open your mind…

On her move to Munich, Germany

Sandy: I felt an internal pull to relocate. I was starting a new life, for example being married. I wanted a fresh new start.

We talked about living in Germany before we got married. I pushed it, thinking it would be new, different, and exciting to experience his culture. So when an opportunity came from his colleague with a valid offer, we went for it. Before that I had only been to France and Austria skiing; during that time we did a short trip to Munich. The most important thing to me was that I felt protected. I wasn't going to be off on my own, but had my husband introducing me to his culture.

I just blindly went. I didn't even look into the culture. I looked a bit into the language, but was just so excited to move overseas, to see what it was like to dive into a foreign country. I went over there blind, thinking it was going to be a lot of fun and exciting every day, more like a vacation than real life. I thought, My husband has a job, I'm going with him, what will be will be. I quit my sales job and thought, How can I be in sales in Germany when I don't speak the language? So I thought about working for an American company overseas.

One of the things I made sure of before going was that Detlef was clear that if I didn't like it we could move back. We set a time limit of two to three years. That was my back door. How naïve! Making an international move is a huge thing, especially for people like us that have a lot of "things" – furniture, etc.

The night that I landed in Munich I experienced immediate culture shock. Detlef was traveling that week. I had to get a taxi to the hotel. I was totally flabbergasted. I felt very vulnerable, very alone. I was scared. There was a convention at the hotel and I went by these women in the hall, shrouded in black cloaks and their entire faces covered, smelling of musk, talking in these shrill tones. I stared at them and they were hissing at me. I was petrified.

I ordered room service and woke up the next day alone and thought, What am I going to do? I don't speak the language. The hotel was a safe haven because people spoke English there. I didn't know where to go or what to do. I wasn't a traveler, but more of a homebody. Even going on the subway was new to me. I had two days alone. It was pretty scary. I bought American magazines. I had my American things around me, toothpaste, shampoo. It sounds trivial but it really makes a difference. I suggest to people to bring something from home that comforts you, like a photo or trinket.

Then Detlef came back and we looked for a place to live with a relocation coordinator. Nothing made sense to me. It took awhile to get the lay of the land. We fell in love with the university sector with international shops and travelers. I thought, This is a good place to start. It was wading in versus jumping off the diving board.

I took a German language course that met every day for three hours. This lasted for months. It was good in that I learned the language. Bad in that everyone in the class was from a foreign country so it was very emotional. Everybody was afraid; no one was themselves. I felt a bonding because we were all in the same situation.

I went through a real down time when I didn't have any friends. The only people I knew were through Detlef's work. I felt very much alone. He was working all day. Starting a new job was a lot of pressure for him. There was a lot of pressure for me learning a new language, new culture, new apartment. A very tense, trying time.

Detlef felt pressure because he had to introduce me to something as simple as grocery shopping. I couldn't read what was on the package. The brand names were different. There was no pre-packaged meat. I had to go through the butcher. I felt extremely inadequate. Even though I started speaking the language a little bit, it was frustrating because I couldn't express myself the way I wanted to. Bavarians are very gruff. Very cold. Not very welcoming. If you can't spit it out…you're in the middle of a city and want a loaf of bread, all you can do is point to it, they pull out the wrong one, there are fifteen people behind you – it's tremendous pressure. Some people would welcome it as a challenge; at that point in my life I wasn't adventurous.

There were too many changes all at once. Making a change can be exciting but as much as you do your homework, it takes time to feel you've landed and you belong. It took me about two years to feel really comfortable. I finally did when I mastered the language to a point I was comfortable, integrated into a job, and was treated like everyone else – not looked upon as "that stupid American."

When I started working my direct boss was American, and I met another American through language class. I just didn't get along with them or have common interests with them. I could either pick these people who were Americans or I was out of luck.

I'm extremely satisfied with my decision to move to Germany. The first two years I was seriously thinking, This isn't going to work, I don't like this; I'm not a city person. It was a culture shock moving from suburbia in the States to a city in Germany. Even people moving from Framingham to Boston experience huge changes. Learning the language, having a job and my own car helped the most. I had freedom and could shop and communicate. I was out with friends after work at the bar, traveling throughout Europe with my company, being independent, learning on my own, versus being dependent on Detlef. This helped him too.

As a result of living in Germany I think I've become much more open-minded to different ways of doing things: with political views, sexuality, trying different foods, everything. Culturally, there's another world out there, not just the U.S. There's so much to see, so many different people; they're all beautiful. It was wonderful to be blessed, to have the opportunity. To be immersed in all that.

The decision to return to the U.S.
Sandy: Throughout our time there I'd always said we'd go back to the States. The longer I stayed in Germany the more integrated I felt. Every year I had milestones of how I changed because every Christmas we came to the States for two and a half weeks. I'd have a real shock of how it is here and constantly made comparisons. At the beginning I started to shun the U.S. I was finding fault with the U.S. and with my home.

In Framingham (Massachusetts) everyone goes to the mall, Super Stop & Shop, and wears what everybody else is wearing. It was culture shock in the opposite direction. Every year I got a real measurement of how I had changed and how inflexible I'd become.

Detlef was offered a job back here near my hometown. It was exciting to think, Wow, a free trip back to the U.S.! They offered relocation with all the perks involved. We sat at dinner and had a heart to heart. We always said we'd come back. We needed to make the decision now. We're going to come back now or wait for the next available opportunity to relocate because it's very costly and a lot of headaches to move yourself. I reluctantly agreed. I wanted to continue to live the fairy tale of living in Germany and have the option of being able to snap my fingers anytime and go back instantly instead of someone snapping their fingers for me saying, "Now or never." It was a difficult decision. At that point I wasn't working, had lost my job, and was down in the dumps, overwhelmed with the thought of having to find another job. I thought, Gee, it's another new beginning back in the U.S.

On returning to the U.S.

Sandy: We came back in 1999. I missed Europe tremendously. I felt the magic kind of went out of life. Everything here was plastic, pre-packaged, commoditized. I felt like I was living in mediocrity. Boston was undergoing construction. It was ugly, dirty. You had Super Stop & Shop, CVS or Walgreen's, no flair, no excitement. I longed to be in Munich where everything was clean. It was like I came from Kodachrome to black and white. I saw that Framingham had progressed but in the wrong direction. I saw it as more negative, more potholes, mediocrity, dirt, crime, restaurants; TGIFs or Ruby Tuesdays, it was so bland.

Detlef: I miss Germany in some ways but I've spent altogether ten to twelve years of my life in the U.S. and by now I definitely feel a sense of belonging over here. We just moved to the town we're in about a year ago, so that's not that easy, but it's improving 'cause we've been here a year. It's getting easier, more integrated now.

How is living in the U.S. feeling seven years later?

Sandy: I've reintegrated into the U.S. It's easier living; everything is so convenient in terms of shopping. You buy a house, you have your land, you have space. Space is important. You have your privacy. It helped that I was close to my family – that was my safe haven – and also finding a job.

It was a culture shock. I'd been in high-tech in Germany, then worked in sales for a cell phone provider here and everything was so much more aggressive and competitive. Roads were busier, stress levels higher. Everyone was maxed out on the credit card, rushing from here to there. You really saw the "keeping up with the Joneses." We were sucked up in that too. Europe is aggressive and competitive but because of six weeks vacation every year, you really get a chance to decompress and relax. The lifestyle is different. You meet friends after work, have dinner, go to an art exhibit. You can do this in the U.S. but living in suburbia again was the reverse of what I had there.

We moved from a very cosmopolitan city to Framingham, Massachusetts with as much class as a bubblegum machine. It was very disappointing. I missed the kaleidoscope of different things. In Munich, every time you turned a corner there was something new to explore. Even in Boston, it's more of the same. They're catering to what they think is in, rather than being creative. Because everyone's the same here the wares tend to be the same. In Europe there are so many different types of people and that was reflected in what was being offered. I think New York is the closest Detlef and I have to being back in Europe. We try to go at least three times a year. It has the same flair as Europe. You can get anything in New York.

Moving to the Cape was another big adjustment. (Moved in 2003) Just this year I feel I'm home. However, I'll never limit myself to saying I'll be here forever. There are so many great experiences. If you're not flexible to wrap your arms around them, you're going to stagnate and not experience some great stuff.

Detlef: The next move would be for private/personal reasons…escaping the weather and…someplace warm where I like the people, the environment, social setting, etc.

Sandy: Home is where the heart is; it's what you make it. Detlef and I are a family unit. I think we could make any place home, just because what's contained inside our windows and doors is us. It might be different from what's happening outside.

Detlef: These relocations make you a different person. I wouldn't want to miss it for the world.

From New York City, London, Tokyo, and Hong Kong to retirement in Bend, Oregon

I'm overjoyed with the way we've retired, including giving back to the community.

– Tim

We moved to a place we could be active. You have to have some reason to get up in the morning other than one more golf game.

– Martha

Tim, in his sixties, from Oregon, is a retired senior executive with Chase Manhattan Bank. Martha, also in her sixties, is from Needham, Massachusetts and co-owner of a firm that places Asian students in U.S. boarding schools. Tim and Martha have moved seventeen times so far, including to New York City, New Jersey, London, Hong Kong, Tokyo, and now Bend, Oregon.

As healthy, active retirees, both Tim and Martha are fully engaged in enjoying as much of life as possible. Very involved in their community, they use Bend as their home base and travel four months of the year.

Martha: In 1991 Tim was with Chase and we started our search while we were living in Hong Kong. Tim had decided he'd retire in his late fifties, in 1996. He's high energy and an avid skier who loves the outdoors. We looked at the Rocky Mountains, ski areas…

Tim: We traveled from Flathead Lake, Montana to Las Cruces, New Mexico. We toured Aspen, Steamboat Springs, Telluride, Sun Valley, Vail, Beaver Creek, and Taos, New Mexico. When we started our search we thought we'd end up in Aspen.

Martha: But Aspen was too glitzy, not for us. We took a two-week trip and stopped in each place trying to imagine ourselves living there. We discovered they were primarily ski towns, not places we could live year-round. We wanted to find a community with people from all walks of life from all over America. We like to ski, hike, ride horses, and play golf. We both like the out of doors, although ironically most of our married life we lived in cities – New York City, London, Tokyo, and Hong Kong.

The best man in our wedding retired to Sisters, a neighboring town of Bend, Oregon, in 1992 and invited us to visit. Tim said he wasn't retiring to Oregon based primarily on high state taxes. But we visited and fell in love with Bend and decided it was where we'd like to retire. The population was only 25,000 in 1992. We were still living in Asia, and spent two years looking for the right combination of property and a home. In December of '94 we bought eighty acres with a view of nine major mountains in the Cascade range. We built a home, turned the property into a working ranch, and retired fully on May 1, 1998.

What we love about Bend is that it's a real community; it's mixed, including all economic levels. It's exploded from 25,000 in 1992 to over 80,000 people in 2006. We have fabulous recreational opportunities. Tim skied seventy-two days last year. Mt. Bachelor, which is a very family-oriented mountain, is only twenty-five minutes away and is within a national forest so there're no commercial buildings or houses. Our weather is fabulous with 275 days of sun a year and nine inches of rain. Because of the wonderful weather, we are able to ride our horses and play golf at one of the thirty-two golf courses within an hour of Bend.

Bend also has unbelievable restaurants. Restaurateurs move here for the quality of life, the recreation. Over 40 percent of the people who live in Bend telecommute. It's attracted a phenomenal group of people who are well-traveled, well-educated, and own second and third homes.

We've never looked back and can't imagine living anywhere else. We're here eight months of the year and travel four. We also own a condo in Vero Beach, Florida and spend about six weeks a year there. We didn't move here saying we hope we'd meet a lot of people and have a lot of close friends. We have a lot of close friends all over world. We wanted to meet people who were at the same educational level and with the same desire to travel.

Tim: We run five hundred acres of a farming operation. I'm on and off tractors everyday. We have three acres of gardens.

Martha: I have friends who are very intellectual, academic, that moved to a community near Jackson Hole, Wyoming, known for its unbelievable recreational opportunities. They found out they had no kindred spirits there. Even worse, they had to shovel snow from September to July. They eventually moved to a more suitable location.

Tim: The more options you have in life the more difficult it is to make a decision. We could have retired in Aspen, the south of France, Tokyo, Hong Kong. We wanted to move to a community that's growing, with colleges and a lot of young people. I don't want to go where everyone dresses the same. If all the men golf and wear pink pants, I don't want to go there.

Now you have a broader perspective of the process and potential outcomes of relocating. In the next chapter you'll hear wisdom and advice from the folks who've relocated, whose quotes and stories you've just read.

Chapter 9: Sharing Their Wisdom

If they had to do it over again…

With some of the moves within Germany I would have done things differently. I sometimes chopped off connections to people I met a bit too abruptly and burned some bridges that way…mainly personal. I did that out of self-protection. I knew I had to move on and I didn't want to live in this world of distant relationships so I cut myself loose every time I moved, and in retrospect I don't think that was such a good idea.

– Detlef, Bourne, Massachusetts

I have no regrets. Even the lows were part of the overall good. You gain strength, learn about yourself, and are forced to grow as a person. Those experiences are just as important as good experiences. They both add to the total package and total positive feeling. If you moved somewhere and everything was rosy you'd be bored. It would be negative. There needs to be a balance. You don't appreciate the good if there's not the bad. If your base of comparison is huge and includes many different experiences, that's great.

– Sandy, Bourne, Massachusetts

I would have rented out my original homestead in New England instead of selling it too quickly.

– Roe, Northern California and Connecticut

I might have secured a job before I got there. It was hard to get one. It took me six weeks.

– Susanne, Denver, Colorado

I might have tried Seattle instead of Miami. As it turned out, Seattle exploded in growth and attention during the '90s, so it would have been a good time to move there. I also love the mountains and the Pacific Northwest. But I'm glad I went to Miami. It was quite an experience.

– Larry, Arlington, Massachusetts

I think I would have taken a little longer to find a job; I took a job real close to my house, but I think I would have taken longer to research the school district.

– Steve, Seattle, Washington

I would have put our house on the market in Massachusetts sooner.

– Michelle, Asheville, North Carolina

I probably would have gotten more familiar with the city first, learning how to find my way around before coming over. I was very young, and never thought about what life would be like coming here. I felt disconnected with the whole moving thing. The only thing I could think of was, Oh, now I can quit my job and go back to China and visit my grandma. After we moved I went to Beijing to stay for three months with my grandma.

– Jennifer, Westborough, Massachusetts

Would I have done anything differently? No, absolutely not. I'm overjoyed with what we've been able to do, including giving back to the community. Martha's mother had a stroke here. They gave her her life back. She would've died if she was in Florida. Instead we had her for another six years.

– Tim, Bend, Oregon

Advice

Go for it! Go with your intuition and it's easier than it would appear to be to do it. Especially as people get older they get more set in their ways and tend to focus on all the reasons why they can't do it, but it's really not as big a drama as people would make it out to be.

– Joe, Seattle, Washington

Go west! Go to the water! Go to the mountains!

– Bob, Cleveland, Ohio

Visit. Possibly meet people who have moved from other areas; find out how they feel about it. Definitely follow up on names of people and phone numbers you've been given. Doing Barbara's workbook helped us to see what we were looking for written down – putting it concretely, black and white, to see that we were going in the right direction...journaling...try to find your inner voice.

– Michelle, Asheville, North Carolina

Do a little research, find something that feels good; then just go for it. I think so many people get stuck job-wise. I understand they need money to pay bills, but so many people are unhappy; it's the little fear thing. Worst case is it doesn't work out, but that's what life is about – experiences. Chalk it up as another learning experience.

– Linda, Asheville, North Carolina

Do it filled with positive thoughts and avoid doing it as a geographical fix. Have positive reasons why you're doing something for yourself, not to remedy other situations that need attention. Engage friends, coworkers, and relatives for names of possible contacts in the new area. Reach out to them, have a tea....don't dump on your old place....join the Y, volunteer somewhere, and get a library card...invite all your family and friends and always send postcards of your new place.

– Roe, Northern California and Connecticut

Follow your bliss. Go to the place; see if it makes you feel comfortable, happy, content, excited, whatever feels good – whatever way it expresses, that's the first thing. Next, go to that area periodically. Get to know it a bit. Scout the area too...But I think the main thing is to follow what makes you feel happy

– Linda C., Cape Girardeau, Missouri

Learn to read your own yes/no signals from your body. You need that in order to experience life in a maximum way. I get energy with "yes" and a lack of energy with "no." I feel heavy when it's not the place for me and I've learned to respond to that quickly instead of "Yes, but I'm supposed to be here; yes, I've made a commitment." Examine that. If it's truly a responsibility I'll fulfill it then I'll get the hell out as fast as I can. Your body speaks true what's right for you. I think it responds very well to the ambience around you.

– Genie, Palo Alto, California

Go with your first gut feeling when you go to the place. Do you say "Wow"? Does it make you feel good inside, happy?

– Steve, Seattle, Washington

It has to feel right. It absolutely has to feel right when the offer comes up. If there are any buts or ifs, it's time to take out the old drawing board. Moving is great because you have the experience…if there was a scale of comfort from 1 to 100, you have to have more than 50-70 to move. If your mother is dying, obviously it's not the right time to move. If there's a good offer and you have no ties, and could advance what you want in life, go. If there is no valid reason to stay, why not take the opportunity?

– Helen, Rancho Palos Verdes, California

You have to follow your heart. You have to look outside your comfort zone. Because change can be a wonderful, positive thing. I think people are afraid of change because it can complicate your life, mix it up. If you're thinking about it, I'd say go and check it out, and see if you get a gut feeling to "Could I live here or not?" People would say to me, "I wish I could do it (relocate)." I'd ask "Why don't you?" They'd say, "Because I have to work." I'd respond, "Well I do too; you just get a job once you get there." It's a gut feeling. When I go to Vale or New York City I say, "I could live here in two seconds." When I go to Idaho or Kansas City, Missouri I feel like "Get me the hell out of here."

– Susanne, Denver, Colorado

Visit the place first to make sure you like it. Then do research on the area, the people, and the job market. Getting a job you like is key to your happiness and success. Also, being comfortable with the local people, and liking them, is very important. And finally make sure you are definitely ready to make a change and leave behind what you now have.

– Larry, Arlington, Massachusetts

Follow your heart. Think about something down the road, three years, five years. What's going to happen as result of this move? Ignore short-term setbacks; look at the next three to five years and see what kind of benefit it'll bring to you. When I moved from Austin to Boston seven years ago, I felt definitely it was the right move. Short-term setbacks can be overcome.

– Bruce, Westborough, Massachusetts

Grab the opportunity as it comes. Never be afraid of making changes, but do research before making that decision. Know the city well. If relocation is for a job, search the industry in which you are going to work in the new city. Know the styles in the new city. For example, from Boston or New York City to rural North Carolina, know the differences. Be familiar with culture shock. Be prepared for a different style of life.

– Jennifer, Westborough, Massachusetts

I think there has to be a reason; you need to fully understand the reason and never lose sight of what that is. Don't let something sidetrack you. For example, we decided to move to the Cape since our goal was to be near the water. Realize and prioritize your goals. If you have to make compromises, make sure they're not dragging you too far from your goal. Any person can make any place home. You could live in a tent and make that place home. People are adaptive. I don't think people should search for their happiness by where they're living. It helps, but there isn't a perfect place in the world. Be open to change. Don't expect it to be easy. Just because it's not easy doesn't mean it's the wrong decision. Accept that. It's not about the goal. The exciting part is the adventure of getting there. All the little hassles, decisions – it's the tapestry of where you are. Don't shun the bad stuff. Live through it; experience it.

– Sandy, Bourne, Massachusetts

I think an important thing is attitude. There's a story about a guy who moved to a new city and sat on park bench. He talked to an older person there, and asked, "How are the people in this city; are they open and welcoming? Will I be happy here? "How were the people in your old city?" the older man replied. "They were great, kind and friendly." "It's the same here," the old man said. The next day another man moved to this city and sat on the same park bench where he met the old man. "I wonder how the people are in this city; are they open and welcoming? Will I be happy here?" "How were the people in your old city?" the older man asked. "They were horrible. Cold and unfriendly." "Oh, well you'll find that they're that way here as well." Moral of the story: It's what you project. If you have positive expectations, you'll make them happen.

– Detlef, Bourne, Massachusetts

My advice to someone who's retiring and thinking of relocating: First you need to decide what your lifestyle is going to be. If you're in your mid-fifties to mid-sixties you'll be retired for a long time if you're lucky health-wise. You want to be as active as possible to maintain your physical capabilities. Plan to have more than one thing to do. If it's just golf, you'll be bored over thirty years. You need to think of medical needs as you get older. If you travel, you need an airport nearby. You also want to move into a community where you can afford to live. Retirement is a lot more complicated than people think it is. Most people who retire probably haven't spent enough time volunteering or giving money to the community they're in. These are often business executives who don't have the time, but when you retire…small communities need help. There are many things you can do to be of assistance even if it's just the United Way or Red Cross. I have too many friends that retire to the golf course and martinis at noon. They're dead in five years.

– Tim, Bend, Oregon

You need to research as best you can where you're going to live. We moved to a place where we could be active. You have to have something else, some reason to get up in the morning other than one more golf game… I would also tell spouses that it's very important for the wife not to put her life on hold in retirement. The woman needs to be sure to continue having a life of her own as well.

– Martha, Bend, Oregon

In closing . . .

Wow! Great advice, huh?

We've now come to the end of our virtual relocation journey together. I applaud you for completing this relocation guide. It has required a large time commitment and dedication on your part, as well as the willingness and ability to go inward, and at times, dig deep. My hope is that what you have learned through this guidebook will help you create more of what you want in all aspects of your life.

And remember, life is about the journey, not the destination. The final chapter provides resources to support you in your journey. Happy travels!

Chapter 10: Resources

Bibliography

Adrienne, Carol and James Redfield. *The Purpose of Your Life: Finding Your Place in the World Using Synchronicity, Intuition, and Uncommon Sense.* New York: Eagle Brook, 1998.

Fritz, Robert. *Path of Least Resistance: Learning to Become the Creative Force in Your Own Life.* New York: Ballantine Books, 1989.

Jeffers, Susan. *Feel the Fear and Do It Anyway.* New York: Fawcett Columbine, 1987.

Keirsey, David. *Please Understand Me II: Temperament, Character, Intelligence.* Del Mar: Prometheus Nemesis Book Company, 1998.

Tieger, Paul D. and Barbara Barron-Tieger. *Do What You Are: Discover the Perfect Career for You Through the Secrets of Personality Type.* Boston: Little, Brown and Company, 1995

Recommended Reading

Callings: Finding and Following an Authentic Life – Gregg Levoy

Excuse Me, Your Life Is Waiting – Lynn Grabhorn

Feel the Fear and Do It Anyway – Susan Jeffers, Ph.D.

Path of Least Resistance: Learning to Become the Creative Force in Your Own Life – Robert Fritz

Places Rated Almanac – David Savageau & Geoffrey Loftus

The Power of Place – Winifred Gallagher

The Purpose of Your Life: Finding Your Place in the World Using Synchronicity, Intuition, and Uncommon Sense – Carol Adrienne

Online Resources

CityRating.com, www.cityrating.com. A comprehensive resource of city demographic guides, local weather forecasts, cost of living, population statistics, crime statistics, school rankings, career and occupational outlook, weather history, average temperatures, relative humidity and general relocation information about the most prominent metro areas in the U.S.

CNN Money - Best Places to Live,
http://money.cnn.com/magazines/moneymag/bplive/2006/. Gives a lot of great information on the best places to live in the U.S., including by state, the top 100, top-earning cities, comparing cities, etc.

Dowsing article, http://www.hlla.com/reference/dowsing.html. Explains more about the "Map Dowsing" exercise found in Chapter 6.

FindYourSpot.com, www.findyourspot.com. A great Internet resource for relocation information and services. You can take their online quiz, and they'll instantly give you a tailored list of places to live in the U.S. that fit your personal style and needs.

George Ward, www.ntastrology.org. Astrocartographer (a professional astrologer who overlays your computerized astrological chart onto a country or world map). A meridian system is used to determine the various astrocartographical influences present at different locations. Phone: 919-231-6500

International Cost of Living Calculator,
http://www.salaryexpert.com/index.cfm?fuseaction=COLCalculator.intlcol&lang=en

International Living Magazine,
http://www.internationalliving.com/issues/2007/2007_article.html. A leading resource for helping people live, travel, and prosper overseas.

Licia Berry, www.liciaberry.com. Spiritual counselor/teacher quoted in Chapter 4.

Moving.com, www.moving.com. Gives you information on moving services, real estate, mortgages, storage, insurance, etc.

Sperling's Best Places, www.bestplaces.net. Provides data on thousands of metro areas, cities, and neighborhoods. You can enter your personal preferences to find your own best place and take the online quiz.

Coach with Barbara!

Do you need help in making your ideal place a reality? Call 828-350-9300 to set up a complimentary consultation or visit my website to learn about my services: www.mycoachbarbara.com

Printed in the United States
150589LV00002B/182/A